YOU SHALL
BE HOLY

YOU SHALL BE HOLY
BE HOLY

Spiritual Basics

TONY PHILPOT

kevin mayhew

First published in 2003 by
KEVIN MAYHEW LTD
Buxhall, Stowmarket, Suffolk IP14 3BW
E-mail: info@kevinmayhewltd.com

© 2003 Tony Philpot

9 8 7 6 5 4 3 2 1 0

ISBN 1 84417 029 2
Catalogue No 1500570

Cover design by Angela Selfe
Edited by Andrew Moore
Typesetting by Louise Selfe

Printed and bound in Great Britain

Contents

About the Author

Tony Philpot is a priest of the East Anglia Diocese, ordained in 1959. He was educated at Bedford School and at the Gregorian University in Rome. He has extensive parish experience in Bedford, Northampton, Leighton Buzzard, Ipswich, Newmarket and Cambridge. For five-and-a-half years he served the Jesus Caritas Priests' Fraternity as what the French call their *Responsable International* (there isn't a comfortable English translation). This meant travelling to all five continents and visiting those groups of priests whose inspiration for living the Gospel is drawn particularly from the life and writings of Charles de Foucauld. He has given retreats in most parts of England, and some overseas. He has written two books on the priesthood, *Brothers in Christ* and *Priesthood in Reality*, and one on Holy Week, *The Cross of Hope*. Since 1997 he has been seconded to work in Italy, and is at present Spiritual Director at the English College in Rome.

Foreword

The business of being alive is the business of understanding our relationship with God, and then living it. Getting a handle on this is not always easy. We need some initial help, a few pointers. That is what this book, with humility, attempts to give. The chapters which follow were originally talks given to men training for the priesthood. The themes of them are, however, quite basic, and common to all. The subtitle of this book is 'Spiritual Basics': there is nothing here which applies exclusively to priests.

So, there are sections here on prayer, our connection with God, the ground of our being who has created and redeemed us; on commitment; on radical unselfishness; on trusting; on living in freedom rather than slavery. There is a chapter on the Holy Spirit, who is given to us without any engineering on our part, and makes all the things in this paragraph possible, not pipe-dreams but really possible. There is a section on our own experience of Jesus, because he is the indispensable focus of our religious life, and needs sharp outlines, not fuzzy ones. There are some reflections on how the Church fits into all of this, and we fit into it, so that we are not Christians-in-a-vacuum, but Christians in the context God has provided, which is his family, chosen and called and reaching out to those who do not yet believe; and two chapters on the Eucharist, two facets of the many-faceted diamond. The talk about the motherhood of Mary is an attempt to sidestep the dutiful pieties one sometimes encounters, and to show how real she is, and how she belongs to the human development of ordinary people like you and me.

I wrote this in Rome, where Pope John Paul II frequently beatifies and canonises people of renowned holiness, and more often than not on a Sunday there will be a new portrait hanging from the balcony of St Peter's – a saint, signed and sealed, flapping in the breeze, as the squads of 'sampietrini' swoop into the piazza and begin to tidy away the thousands of plastic chairs. Some people are critical of the sheer volume of saint-making. It seems to me, however, that in our cynical, sour and debunking days it is good that the Pope should point often to individuals and say, 'Now, here's a really good person.' It can be done. Not everyone is corrupt, there are not skeletons in every cupboard, he is saying. By the grace of God, and not otherwise, holiness is actually possible.

However many people are 'raised to the altars', they are the tiniest fraction of the human race. Holiness must be more widely available than this. We can't leave it to the founders and foundresses of movements and religious orders. And holiness is not the same as piety. Most of us could not be pious to save our lives. Holiness is something much more substantial, much more muscular, and much more ordinary.

I would like to thank Fr Andrew Moore for his considerable work in editing this book, and the men at the English College in Rome for being very patient listeners to a rather idiosyncratic spiritual director.

Tony Philpot
Rome, 2002

1

Holiness

When God speaks to Moses in Leviticus 19, and gives him a message for the whole people of Israel, it starts with a bang. 'You shall be holy, for I the Lord your God am holy.' Here is the most basic requirement that God makes of us. Then comes the small print. The small print is fascinating, because it jumbles up our duty to God and our duty to neighbour. You can't really pluck them apart. If you are a pious person, but a cold-hearted bastard to your neighbour, then your piety is a fake. Holiness involves both at once.

Holiness means, in the first place, discovering how to pray, and becoming a person of prayer. The process is different from that of learning facts or opinions. Learning facts and opinions is to do with the head. Prayer is to do with the heart. To discover how to pray is an awakening of the heart, a schooling of the heart. It takes longer to school the heart than it does the head. In his Spiritual Canticle, John of the Cross says, 'There are depths to be fathomed in Christ. He is like a rich mine with many recesses containing treasures, and no matter how men try to fathom them the end is never reached.'* But at least we can reach the beginning. Timothy Radcliffe, in his recent book *Sing a New Song*, says, 'Contemplation of the only-begotten Son is the root of all mission . . . without this stillness there is no movement.'† In *Novo Millennio Ineunte*, the Pope says, 'The great mystical tradition of the Church of both east and west . . . shows how prayer can progress, as a genuine dialogue of love, to the point of rendering

---

* St John of the Cross, 'Spiritual Canticle' translated by Allison Peers (1935), taken from *The Complete Works of St John of the Cross* (Anthony Clarke)
† Timothy Radcliffe, *Sing a New Song* (Dominican Publications, 1999)

the person wholly possessed by the Divine Beloved, vibrating at the Spirit's touch, resting filially within the Father's heart.'* This must be our goal. To vibrate at the Spirit's touch. Nothing less will do.

Holiness means, simultaneously, treating other people right. We all have in us reservoirs of contempt, of derision, of revulsion, of prejudice of one kind or another. We are all capable of being clever and cutting at the expense of others: it is only too easy. You remember, perhaps, that passing remark of Samuel Butler: 'How good of God to let Carlyle and Mrs Carlyle marry one another, and so make two people miserable instead of four.' My first instinct is to say, 'That's brilliant – I wish I'd said it.' My second, however, is to say, 'That remark is amusing, and makes me laugh, but it's unkind and unchristian.' Well, it took me years to learn that. It is a slow business, draining the contempt, the derision, the revulsion, the prejudice and that acid smartness out of us. It is the business of holiness.

Holiness means finding out how to love. Love is not primarily a question of feelings. It is a matter of the will, of the decision. Nevertheless, true love is tender, and considerate, and all the things Paul says in 1 Corinthians 13. Patient and kind, rejoicing in the truth, bearing all things, believing all things, hoping all things, enduring all things. I remember a middle-aged Polish chap, 40 years ago. He was married to an English woman with a progressive illness. She was bedridden, and totally paralysed except for the muscles of her neck and mouth, dependent on an artificial respirator, needing to be fed in tiny spoonfuls. He waited on her night and day. His married life, physically speaking, was over: the consolations of marriage. But the example of love that he gave was powerful beyond words. The heart is stronger than the feelings, is more than the feelings. Growing into this, growing into the living of real charity, is the business of holiness.

---

* Encyclical of John Paul II, *Novo Millennio Ineunte* (2001), paragraph 33

Holiness means putting on Christ. It means training ourselves to be real disciples, carrying our cross with him. We recoil from the Cross. In theory, fine; we know the theory. In practice we fail to see life's incidental sufferings as providential, so that we can now become real disciples, carrying the Cross. It is a slow affair, shouldering the Cross.

The school of holiness works at a slower pace than the purely intellectual one. We have to be very patient. At a recent Consistory, Pope John Paul quoted Newman. Newman, accepting his nomination as Cardinal, said, 'Christianity has been too often in what seemed deadly peril, that we should fear for it any new trial now. Commonly the Church has nothing more to do than to go on in her own proper duties, in confidence and peace, to stand still and see the salvation of God.' This splendid old man, back in 1879, was speaking from his own experience. He was saying, in effect, 'Times are tough; religion is under siege; the Church has her back to the wall; but it's all happened before, and we have only to do our duty before God, and he will look after us.' At the time he was 78 years old. He knew how long it had taken him to learn this, to learn to carry out the task the Lord had given him with confidence and with peace, remaining steadfast and tranquil, patiently awaiting the salvation of God. To grow into this state of mind is a life's work. In the matter of holiness, there are no quick fixes.

In the same Consistory homily the Pope said, 'The Church does not rely on calculation and human power, but on Christ Crucified, and on the coherent testimony rendered to him by the apostles, martyrs, and confessors of the faith.' That word 'coherent' sounds strange to English ears; it is a very Italian word, *coerente*. It means 'following through'; it means 'putting your money where your mouth is'; it means 'working on until the job is finished'. It makes us think of Jesus' warning to his friends: 'Not everyone who says to me, "Lord, Lord," will enter the kingdom of heaven, but only the one who does the will of my Father in heaven' (Matthew 7:21). To become coherent in the service of God is a life's work.

The Devil will do his best to distract you from your resolution to take the path of holiness. One of the things he will
try to do is make you a partisan. It is natural that we should
have strong feelings about things. You may have fire in your
belly about justice in the world. You may have great zeal for
orthodox belief in the Church. You may be enthusiastic
about properly conducted liturgy. You may have the strongest
possible sentiments about the sanctity of human life, from
the womb to the grave. You may care enormously about
Christian unity. Indeed, all these things should be the concern
of all of us, if we are true children of the Church. Your
emphasis and mine, however, will differ according to our
character, experience and background. We will give ourselves,
and others too, labels: progressive, traditional, conservative
and liberal. There is nothing here to distress us unduly, for
there has always been difference of opinion in the Church.
When the Devil does take a hand, however, is when we
become campaigners for our cause in such a way that the
campaign becomes a substitute for the spiritual life. The
Devil takes a hand when he encourages us to write people
off, dismiss them, because of a remark they have made or
even because of a mistake they have made. Your prime aim,
however, must be union with Jesus Christ. There is no other
prime aim worth having.

Spelt out like this it all sounds rather daunting. Don't be
daunted. You can't do it all at once. Be merciful to yourself,
be patient. But realise that every day is given to you so that,
by God's grace, you may make a small advance. Nothing is
wasted. The attempt to pray, even for a short while. The
gesture of good-humoured service to someone else, however
minute. The human overtures made to someone with a different
theological stance. The ache or pain accepted in union with
Jesus on the Cross. Each new day bristles with chances, some
of which we will seize, and some not. So long as there is
movement, that's all right. Movement in prayer and movement
in charity. There are times, I know, when it feels like an uphill

grind on a drab day, and we wonder what on earth we're doing. It's our tenacity and our faithfulness on those days which are the solid gold of holiness. 'I cannot see the distant scene; one step enough for me,' to quote Newman again. What's sinister is when the movement stops, either because we are smug and self-satisfied, or because we have despaired. So this call to holiness is not meant to depress; it is meant to encourage. It is meant to help in focusing on the raw material of holiness, and, however gradually, claim it for your own.

2

Black Holes and Discus Throwers

I am scientifically illiterate. But someone once explained black holes to me in these terms. Floating around the universe there are larges masses of matter, perhaps of the dimension of planets, or even bigger, and for some reason these shrink in size. They become more and more dense as they become smaller, until the field of gravity with which they surround themselves is quite irresistible, extraordinarily strong. In this state they attract everything to them, like magnets. And because their gravity pull is so great, nothing escapes from them. Not even light! This is why they are called black holes.

There is a parallel in the spiritual life. When the Church, or Scripture, talks to us about sin, they are really talking about black holes. Because all sinfulness is a variation on a theme. The theme is our using people and things in a selfish way, pulling them to ourselves and giving little or nothing back. Which is exactly what a black hole does.

One of the loveliest pieces of sculpture on earth is the Greek statue, by Myron, of the Discus Thrower. The artist has brought out the sublime, unselfconscious beauty of the human body. The discus thrower, too, has a spiritual parallel. Imagine the act of throwing the discus. In the statue, the arm holding the discus is at rest, dangling by the athlete's side. But now imagine the arm flexed right back to the shoulder, like a tautened spring, awaiting the precise moment of release. Imagine the power with which he propels the discus into the air, the exact angle he chooses. Picture the discus cutting the air in a long, shallow parabola, almost floating above the grass for the last few metres, and the gasp of the crowd once they see the power of the throw. Now reflect. The discus thrower has put every ounce of his strength, every fibre of his being, you might say, into projecting the discus outwards, away from himself. He is the opposite of a black hole. His entire energy is dedicated to a movement which is out, away, beyond. And this is how a truly unselfish person behaves. His whole *raison d'être* is to be *for* God, *for* others. He is unself-conscious, like the discus thrower. And all holiness is a variation on this theme.

We can illustrate all this from our own experience. I suppose the most damaging sins – damaging, that is, in the extent of their result – are pride and resentment. For the saving of face and the avenging of slights, people have been willing to wage wars, to enslave and kill thousands. If you analyse their state of mind, you find the perfect example of the black hole. The proud person is so conscious of their rank and dignity and the respect which is due to them that they spend all their ingenuity protecting and enhancing their power. This is now recognised to be so much a part of public life that it is presumed, in the press, that every public figure is single-mindedly intent on achieving promotion, honour and power, and that that's why they're in politics anyway. Hitler and Stalin were paranoid maniacs, willing to sacrifice thousands to protect themselves from any kind of threat, real or imaginary. Rightly, we condemn them. Yet at the same time, today, the members of the cabinet are put under the microscope by the media to see who is jostling for position. The College of Cardinals, the media take for granted, is full of men who want nothing more than to become Pope, and will intrigue and manoeuvre to bring this about. Are they all black holes, pulling everything and everyone into their orbit to serve their own purposes and advantage? The only difference is, the public presumes, that the methods they use are more respectable and gentle. But, interestingly, public opinion does not blame public figures for their presumed ambition, nor for their ruthlessness: in a way, it admires them. What an awful pattern of social existence this is! If society has to be full of people who walk on others' faces, however nicely, in order to achieve supremacy, what hope is there for any of us? Where is unselfishness? Where is the desire to build up, to help, to remedy, to create? I believe, for what it is worth, that the media have it wrong. I believe that there are many people, both men and women, who are not exploiters, and who are net givers, net contributors; who are willing to step down and make way for others; who are, in their own way, discus throwers. Thank God that this is so. I am no great defender of the system which produced the landed gentry in England. The story of the agricultural poor in our country, over the centuries, is not a pretty one. But some of the landowners have a feeling for their estates which transcends selfishness, and which illustrates the point. An elderly lord of the manor may lay down a cellar full of port which he knows will not be ready for drinking before he dies. He will plant a wood of oak trees which will not come to their full maturity for two hundred years. He will spend his money and his devotion on projects like these, knowing the satisfaction they give will never be his. He does it for his heirs. He does it because the land deserves it. In his own eccentric way he is a discus thrower.

But there is enough of the black hole to preoccupy us, both on the world scene and – if we are honest – on the personal one. How often have wars taken place, or continued, so that the stance adopted by a particular nation didn't have to be abandoned? Henry Kissinger said of the recent war in Yugoslavia, 'NATO cannot lose this one,' meaning, 'NATO cannot afford to lose face by backing down once the war has started.' If losing face is the issue, rather than the humanitarian reason for going to war in the first place, then the war has become immoral. You don't, as a Christian, kill people to keep your honour intact. From being, at the start, a discus thrower – spending yourself for the weak and helpless – you have become a black hole, intent only on your reputation, on being perceived as strong and successful. I am not here arguing either for or against the action in Kosovo and Serbia. I am simply pointing out that public opinion very quickly and easily settles for motives of jingoism and pride, and counts this as virtuous, when in fact it is vicious.

The story of the Prodigal Son (Luke 15) is worth studying for the characters in it. The prodigal son starts as a black hole. He goes to his father and rudely demands his money, although it is not yet time for this. He is greedy for cash, and he is oblivious to his father's feelings. He is concerned only with his own advantage and his own pleasure, and is prepared to manipulate others to get his way. Later, having worked his way through his inheritance, he comes to his senses, realises the gravity of his mistake, and plans his return, plans the little speech he will make. Is he at this moment behaving as a black hole or a discus thrower? Is he simply being cunning for his own advantage, or is his penitence sincere? In the story, it's a bit ambiguous, and we are not quite sure. The father, running to meet him, clothing him in the best robe, killing the fatted calf, could have indulged in self-pity and resentment, squeezing yet more abject apologies out of the boy. 'Think of my feelings,' he could have said, 'and so many years without a word from you, and us not knowing if you were alive or dead. It's all very well for you to turn up out of the blue and expect me to take you back . . .' But he doesn't. He refuses to go down that path. In this he differs, I suspect, from many of us. The father is clearly a discus thrower. The implication is that his behaviour is so generous, so unselfish, so willing to forget the past, or at any rate to draw a veil over it, that any mixed motive in the prodigal son is transformed into sincere repentance, and a resolve to live for his father. The elder son, however, *is* full of resentment. So full that one suspects the hurt feelings had been seething under the surface for many years. He believes that he has a grievance, that he has been unjustly treated. Perhaps he is right. But by his response – sulking, and demanding recognition of his hurt feelings – he too becomes a manipulator, and a black hole. And this in spite of the fact that, as he says himself, he has never put a foot wrong. Just causes too easily become the platform for self-centred behaviour.

A few years ago a Mexican film was doing the rounds. It was called *Like Water for Chocolate*. It was about a woman who had three daughters. She was willing to let the first two go – one to a wealthy marriage, one to a thrilling life of extreme politics and rebellion – but the third she kept for herself. It is your duty, she said to her, to sacrifice your life in looking after your mother. The implication on the part of the mother was, 'I deserve this, after giving you the gift of life and bringing you up; it's time for *my* feelings, *my* interests to be taken into account.' The story of the film is the story of how the third daughter deals with the situation. There is lots of entertaining Latin American 'magic realism' in the film, and a great deal of fairly rumbustious humour. We all know, I am sure, of cases where a child very willingly, and without being asked, devotes herself to looking after an ageing parent. This can be a very healthy relationship, with unselfishness and freedom on both sides. But if it topples over into tyranny, where an ageing parent manipulates by shame and pathos, and the result is a kind of slavery in which one person's life is gobbled up by another, then that's the black hole again. The black hole is as present in our individual lives as it is in national or international life. The beautiful reverse of this is the number of ordinary people whose praises are never sung, who good-humouredly and patiently, over long periods of time, forget themselves in the service of God and other people, in the family and out of it. It proves, to me, that the Resurrection has worked; that it has become not just the Resurrection of Christ but the spiritual resurrection of millions of others, some who are consciously his followers and disciples, and others who are not, but all of whom are discus throwers in the full, spiritual sense.

I mention the Resurrection at this stage because Jesus is the best example of all of the discus thrower. He makes apparent to us what has been the case in the Blessed Trinity all along. Each of the Three Persons is only understandable in terms of the other two. Each exists for the other two. The relationship between the three is so important that their identity is, in fact, their relationship. This is hard for us to picture or to grasp. Jesus makes it a bit easier by bringing that same kind of unselfishness on earth, and devoting his life to the Father and to us. 'My food,' he says, 'is to do the will of him who sent me' (John 4:34). And 'No one has greater love than this, to lay down one's life for one's friends' (John 15:13) . . . which is exactly what he was about to do himself. He is the supreme example of the self-forgetful person. He is not a doormat, or creepily subservient. He is a free man, with the dignity of a free man. But he uses that freedom in favour of his Father and of us. 'For those who want to save their life will lose it,' he says (Luke 9:24), 'and those who lose their life for my sake will save it.'

A visit to Rome and its surroundings will provide many examples both of black holes and discus throwers. You will meet evil emperors like Nero, who sacrificed everything and everyone to personal pleasure and satisfaction. The Colosseum was built on land he expropriated, for the kind of public show in which he himself would be the chief performer. You will also meet the anonymous heroes of the catacombs, many of them martyrs, who sacrificed their lives as disciples of the Lord. You will meet St Benedict, who abandoned a life as a hermit and devoted himself to building up a whole new way of Christian community living, although in the process he had to survive several attempts on his life. In the Vatican Museum you will find the most sumptuous rooms of the most self-indulgent popes. One Renaissance pope is supposed to have said, 'Since God has conferred the Papacy upon us, let us enjoy it.' In the English College, on the other hand, you will find the list of young martyrs who, mostly in the same century, offered their whole brief existence so that the beleaguered Catholics in the days of persecution should not be deprived of Mass and sacraments. One, Ralph Sherwin, when asked whether he was ready at the end of his studies to return to England and labour for the salvation of souls – with all the attendant risks to himself – replied, '*Potius hodie quam cras*' – 'Today rather than tomorrow.'

This analogy, of black holes and discus throwers, can become tedious. I am sure there are many others, and better ones, which could be used. But for what it's worth, let's make this our prayer, just for today: 'Dear Lord, make me a discus thrower.'

3

Risk

When I was ordained, my uncle, who was a priest in the Arundel and Brighton Diocese, came to grace the occasion and keep me company on the sanctuary, as was the custom, during the ordination Mass at St John Lateran. When later in the day I went to visit him at his hotel I was astonished to find him standing on a chair with his head in the lavatory cistern. Had it all been too much for him, I wondered. No – he had a golden rule when checking into a foreign hotel. 'Always check the ball-cock in the cistern,' he said. 'Defective plumbing could wreck your holiday.'

Other people have other priorities. Some folk need, as the very first imperative, to discover and inspect the fire escapes, and to make sure that all the doors really open. These you might describe as the belt-and-braces people. (If they are male, that is.) Belt-and-braces is a way of being. It means taking every precaution so that you cannot blame yourself for being careless if something happens. It means being in control, as far as humanly possible, of your own destiny. It means keeping the reins in your hands, because who knows what would happen otherwise. It means being good at DIY, very often, because only if you do all your own DIY can you be sure that the materials are the right ones and the job has not been skimped. In its extreme forms, belt-and-braces reduces you to a kind of paralysis. A wife asks her husband to fix the family up with a cheap and cheerful off-season holiday. He goes to the travel agent and gets the brochures, and they look through them together. The choice is not easy to make, because all the places look the same. Whether they are in Turkey, or Ibiza, or Sicily, multi-storey modern hotels (chalk-white) with kidney-shaped swimming pools (stunning blue) are identical; so are the bronzed people sipping their Daiquiris under the palm trees. So what does he do? He goes for security. Which airline has the best safety record in the air? Not easy to establish, as a lot of these trips are run by charter firms, which come and go like mushrooms in the wet grass. So he decides to find out who the firms belong to, who has shares in them. This one belongs to a supermarket chain. What do grocers know about safety at 35,000 feet? This one belongs to a newspaper baron, but of course newspapers sell best when there has been a disaster. This one was founded on the smoking ruins of a previous one which went bankrupt, leaving hundreds of passengers stranded at Dubrovnik: hardly a recommendation. While he is doing the research (midnight oil on the internet) all the cheap trips are sold out, and the family ends up in a draughty tent on the outskirts of Yarmouth.

I do not want to make fun of careful people. Careful is a perfectly proper way to be. My personal tendency would be to take the chance and buy the tickets, but that is probably because I am naturally careless and impatient with details, and will one day be caught with neither belt nor braces. My way, too, is a fairly common way of being. Neither camp has the right to criticise the other. Adverting to the contrast between types, however, brings to the surface the subject of *risk*. Is risk, for you, a dirty word? Or is it an exciting, enlivening word? Do you put it on the sin side of the ethical divide, or on the virtue side? Our rather puritanical vocabulary attaches a slur to words like 'chancer', 'gambler', and phrases like 'short-cut'. They suggest someone who is morally defective.

And yet, the whole of our spiritual life involves risk, in the sense that it involves letting the controls out of your own hands, and surrendering yourself to somebody else. Only God has heaven in his gift. Neither you nor I can earn it. I remember an old priest being asked by his sister-in-law, none too delicately, what he meant to happen to his money when he died. 'I've put it all into Masses,' he answered, 'to be said for my soul.' They were standing on a pier at the time, for reasons which for the moment escape me, and she was so shocked that she nearly fell into the sea. She was shocked for the wrong reason. She had hoped to inherit his cash. Yet you wonder about the old priest, don't you? What did he really believe about God? That a multitude of Masses would appease God more than just one? Was he, perhaps, putting a safety net under himself, so that he could say to God at the judgement, 'You can't touch me – I have a foundation Mass being said for me once a month at Felpingham-on-Sea.' Did he really believe that God was his loving Father, or did he feel the need for some ammunition just in case he wasn't? It would be wrong of me to judge. But I do know that sooner or later all of us have to surrender ourselves into the Father's hands, take the risk, trust that he is and will be merciful, put all our eggs in this basket and no other. Only God has heaven in his gift, and it *is* a gift. We, who are accustomed to earning everything we have, see this almost as an issue of self-respect. We have a whole battery of sayings which express this, like 'You'll not get owt for nowt' and 'There's no free lunch'. Our faith teaches us however that you *will* get owt for nowt, and that there *is* a free lunch. Grace is what it says, gratuitous, free, a sheer gift, and glory is the continuation of grace. All God asks is that we take the risk, jump into his arms, and say, 'I trust you.'

Listen to Ignatius Loyola. This is a prayer I have always found very powerful.

> Take, O Lord, into your hands
> my entire liberty.
> Receive my memory, my understanding and my whole will.
> All that I have, all that I am,
> comes from you
> and I give it back again to you
> to be disposed of according to your good pleasure.

Give me but your love and your grace.
With these I am rich enough
and wish for nothing more.

With that mentality you could move through life with a light heart.

I remember, back in the 1950s, a brilliant young professor at the Gregorian University in Rome called Juan Alfaro, who taught us about faith. Faith, he used to say, is essentially obscure. In other words, it is never founded on evidence which is absolutely compelling. If this were the case it would not be faith any more, but simply an unavoidable intellectual conclusion. Room has to be left for an act of generosity on the part of the believer. John of the Cross said something similar. He said that you come to God by a negative path. You can say easily what God is not. It is much harder to say what he is. When we try to look at God the light is so bright that it blinds us, and the effect is that all we see is darkness, opaqueness. The eyes of our mind cannot encompass God. This side of the grave he will never be intellectually satisfying. We can only know him and contact him with the heart, with what the Italians would call the *slancio* of the heart, and what the French would call the *élan* of the heart. It's what a child does when out with his dad: he jumps off the garden wall and says, 'Catch me,' never doubting that he will be safe. And, of course, he is safe. Some people find trusting harder than others.

Risk is an integral element in our religion. This is not surprising. Think of the risk Our Lady took when she said, 'Be it done unto me according to thy word.' You will say, 'But it wasn't really a risk, because she knew that God would make it all OK,' and maybe that is true up to a point, but it would be quite wrong to downgrade the heroism of her choice. It was, for her, a jump out of security into the perilous unknown. Think of the risk Our Lord took in Gethsemane when he said, 'Let this chalice depart from me, but not my will but thine be done.' You will say, 'But it wasn't really a risk, because he knew that his Father would never abandon him, and that he would rise again at Easter.' True up to a point, but not to the point of saying, 'He wasn't really frightened, he was just pretending.' He wasn't pretending at all; he was petrified with terror, and this is where the heroism of his choice comes from. The Father allowed him to experience the paralysing fear of painful annihilation, and he took the risk of saying 'Yes' to whatever the Father wanted. There was no safety net under either Mary or Jesus. They both took the risk.

It's true of marriage, isn't it? And maybe this is the reason why so many people don't get married. To tie yourself to another human being for the rest of your life is a risk, and there are an awful lot of belt-and-braces people out there, of both sexes. It is a risk taken in love and in trust: a three-cornered risk, where you say to your husband or wife, 'I will be true to you under all circumstances,' and in the same breath you say to God, 'I trust you to help me keep this promise.' And God says to you, 'Take the plunge, take the risk, and I will care for you whatever happens.' Generosity begets generosity. A step taken in faith invokes God's mercy as nothing else does. When you marry you sign a blank cheque on the future, but whatever happens God will be there for you.

Well, the same is true about ordination. A prospective ordinand might say, 'It's a risk. What if I found I couldn't get on with the Parish Priest? What if I fell in love with the barmaid at the Goat and Compasses? What if I found I was short on job satisfaction? What if the cook insisted on serving me spinach, which I can't stand?' All these things are distinct possibilities. But a God who left him alone in such circumstances and did not come to his aid would hardly be a God worth serving anyway, would he? Men become priests precisely in order to proclaim to the world a God of mercy and tenderness, a God who has revealed himself as Father – in other words, the God of Jesus Christ. The God of Jesus

Christ responds infallibly to a risk taken in faith. To say 'Yes' to ordination or to marriage is not to sign a contract with a blank future. It is to sign a contract with a loving Father. If he knows the future, my future, which he does, and *still he calls me*, then the risk is definitely worth taking.

Nobody can force you to take the risk. It will always be a personal decision. It is a decision that has to do with generosity of heart. On the one side there is the temptation to say, 'What if?' But on the other, *'Duc in altum'*, launch out into the deep, says the Holy Father in *Novo Millennio Ineunte*,* quoting St Luke; get out of your depth as you did on the first day you actually learned to swim. 'These words,' he says, 'ring out for us today, and they remind us to remember the past with gratitude, to live the present with enthusiasm and to look forward to the future with confidence.' It isn't a question of committing yourself imprudently and thought-lessly to a way of life you are not suited to: that would be stupid. It is a question of having the courage to say 'Yes' to an invitation from the God Peter describes to us in his first Letter (1 Peter 1:8):

> Although you have not seen him, you love him;
> and even though you do not see him now,
> you believe in him and rejoice
> with an indescribable and glorious joy,
> for you are receiving the outcome of your faith,
> the salvation of your souls.

---

* Encyclical of John Paul II, *Novo Millennio Ineunte* (2001), paragraph 58

4

Prayer

In Romans 8:26 there is an extraordinary statement. Paul says, 'We do not know how to pray as we ought.' Is he using 'we' to mean 'I'? Does Paul really mean that after all that evangelical activity, and that direct experience of God on the road to Damascus, and his time in the desert, he actually does not know how to pray? If so, what hope is there for us?

The context is his reflection on the awesome deed of God, what he has done for us in the wake of the Resurrection. God has rescued us from a life of futility, a life of impotence and aimlessness, a life of going round in sinful circles. He has lifted us clear of all that and established us in the kingdom of his Son. He has filled us with the Spirit. So even if we by ourselves 'do not know how to pray as we ought', now the Spirit inside us does the praying for us. Paul is saying that without the Holy Spirit neither he nor we would have a clue how to pray. We would not know the language.

That statement, however – 'We do not know how to pray as we ought' – does echo our own experience on bleary mornings, doesn't it? I honestly do my best. I select a passage from Scripture and read it. I try to compose myself, and to concentrate. The result is half an hour or an hour of distractions, of gritty anxieties floating to the surface, of droppings-off to sleep and wakings-up again. I have to admit that I don't *feel* full of the Spirit. I feel somehow alienated from God – and also a bit ashamed, because after all these years I should be able to do better than this. I ask myself, 'Have I been doing it wrong all the time? Should I go back to the beginning and learn the techniques properly?

An expert on prayer and the spiritual life once told me,

'There is only one rule about prayer, and that is – be there.' In other words, I think she meant, turn up. In other words, ring-fence the time. This reminds me of the beginning of John 12, when Mary pours out a fabulous jar of ointment over the feet of Jesus, and Judas is shocked. My equivalent of costly ointment is time. In the modern world, time is the most valuable thing I have. To give it freely to Our Lord is the greatest compliment I can pay him. Having said that, what happens in that time is not as important as I think it is, because the Spirit will be doing the work anyway.

Experts distinguish between different sorts of prayer: liturgical and non-liturgical, communal and private, vocal and mental. I'm not going to waste time on any of that – it's all obvious anyway. There is one distinction which merits a pause, however, and that is the one between discursive and contemplative prayer.

Discursive prayer is often linked to the name of St Ignatius Loyola. Part of the Counter-Reformation, the Catholic Church putting her house in order, was developing working models of prayer that could be used by anyone. The Jesuits very quickly became dominant in the world of those new-fangled and trendy places called 'seminaries', and into them they imported the Ignatian method of prayer. It was still fighting fit 400 years later when I came to the seminary. Every night, as part of night prayer, we would have read to us, in Latin, a meditation by a seventeenth-century Jesuit called Avancinus. We were supposed to go to bed thinking about it, so that we would be ready for the half-hour of silent prayer before Mass the next morning. We called it 'medi', which was short for meditation. Avancinus would take a passage from the Gospel, and methodically employ your imagination, your intellect and your will. He would get you to picture the scene, and put yourself in it – as a bystander, an apostle, a soldier, a scribe. He would encourage you to listen to the words, place yourself by the roadside, or in a boat on the lake of Galilee, or in the square in front of Pilate's palace, to sense the atmosphere, to *feel*. Once you had immersed yourself in the Gospel reality, he would encourage you to make the transition to your own life: I am the one of little faith who sinks in the water; I am the dead one being carried to the cemetery who needs bringing back to life; I am the fickle inhabitant of Jerusalem who shouts, 'Hosanna!' on Sunday and 'Crucify him!' on Friday. All these stories are stories about my life, too. And from this came the third stage, the stage where the heart speaks. It speaks words of sorrow, of hope, of love. Avancinus was not quite sure he could trust us to let our hearts loose unsupervised, so he would tell us the kind of prayers he expected of us: *'Dole, propone, etc.'* – 'Mourn and make good resolutions.' This is good workaday prayer, which anyone can do, even when they are not feeling especially pious. See the wisdom of it. The use of the imagination forestalls the distractions we might otherwise have. The application to modern life involves a salutary dose of reality. The prayer of the heart makes sure that it isn't just a mental game or an intellectual exercise: there is strong communication with God. I used this technique with my RCIA people at the end of every Monday night meeting, just for a quarter of an hour, praying out loud so as to lead them. It was enormously popular and it filled a perceived need. It was as if they had said to me, 'Teach us how to pray', and through this very simple formula I was able to model it for them.

Ignatius was putting his own distinctive mark on a form of prayer which was much older than him. This was called *'Lectio Divina'* – literally, 'Divine Reading'. It was the monks' way of praying at length, outside the framework of the *'Opus Dei'*, the liturgy. It is almost as old as the Church, and Gregory the Great clearly prayed like this and taught his people to do so. However, it was a Carthusian abbot called Guigo, in the twelfth century, who first described it methodically. *Lectio Divina* means praying with Scripture. Scripture is not given to us like a bulletin from the BBC website, full of the latest breaking news. On the contrary, it is the word of God for us, and it stands for ever, because God is its principal author, and it is endowed with a power which goes beyond its utility or literary value. God's word is a vehicle for his Presence, if we let it be. I ought to expand this a bit, so that I do not sound too fundamentalist. Obviously the actual printed book, the individual translation, is not the word of God itself, but a means of bringing it to us – otherwise we would have to claim that the Holy Spirit had inspired the Jerusalem Bible, and had inspired the New Jerusalem *even more*, which is absurd; or else that the Spirit had inspired only the original piece of parchment or paper, and was entirely absent from everything which has happened since, which would seem to defeat the object of inspiration. No, the thing is, when I read Scripture, I do so as a member of the Church, which is Spirit-filled, and the Spirit who fills me is the same as the one who worked through those original writers. I can read what is here 'in the light of the same Spirit by whom it was written'. Let's have a look at the stages in *Lectio Divina*.

To begin with, I *read the text* slowly and reverently. I do this humbly, realising that through it God may communicate with me today in a way he did not do yesterday. This is quite a challenge to me, because in my studies I tend to speed-read in order to inform myself as quickly as I can. Throttling back can be hard. So I try to read attentively, openly and with commitment. St Ambrose says, 'We should read the words not in agitation, but in calm; not hurriedly, but slowly, a few at a time, pausing in attentive reflection . . . Then the reader will experience their power to enkindle the ardour of prayer.' So, be patient.

The next stage is *meditation*. This is less formidable than it sounds. It means that I think the thing through, let it resonate within me like a musical theme which has moved me deeply. God told Ezekiel (3:10-11), 'All my words that I shall speak to you receive in your heart and hear with your ears; then go to the exiles, to your people, and speak to them.' Receive in your heart. I try to digest what I read so that it enters into my bloodstream, my way of being. So I think of the different depths of meaning it contains, and of other texts which it echoes, or which echo it. St Bernard said to his monks, 'Be pure ruminants.' Take it easy. There are no prizes for getting to the tape first. Be patient.

The third stage is *prayer*. Pope John Paul II, in *Novo Millennio Ineunte*, describes how a person can be 'wholly possessed by the Divine Beloved, vibrating at the Spirit's touch.'* When we take on board the living word of God, our heart vibrates at the Spirit's touch, and we want to cry out to God – in praise, in petition, in sorrow, in thanks. It is a natural response. Jean Lafrance, in his last book, *Day and Night*, says that we are by our nature beggars before God, implorers, expressers of need. Before God we have no other status than that of being utterly dependent. So often our reflection upon Scripture makes us once again conscious of this. Everything we say to God – hope and trust for the future, regret for things in the past, concern for those we love – all these things can be prefaced by the one word, 'Please . . .' When we say 'please' we are being most authentically ourselves before God. We should never be ashamed to do this.

And the fourth stage is *contemplation*. It is not wanting to use words any more, not to ask for things any more, moving on from that to be in the company of the Lord in a sustained and wordless way, like Mary, Martha's sister, who sat at his feet in Luke 10:42. It is the point where the prayer begins to pray itself within me. It is a relationship of faith and love between the human soul and God. At this stage the brain goes into hibernation, I cease to assess myself or the quality of my prayer – I am simply there, with him and for him. I am aware of his presence to me, *'intimior intimo meo'*, as Augustine said – 'closer to me than I am to myself'. It is a form of prayer which is utterly simple. I go down inside myself until, at the very depth of my being, at the key point of my identity as a person, I find the Lord, whose indwelling

---

* Encyclical of John Paul II, *Novo Millennio Ineunte* (2001), paragraph 33

in me since baptism is a theological fact. Here I face God without my masks, without all the disguises and personae that I put on in order to live with my fellows. Here I am who I really am, and with this naked, primitive, original self I face God, and know myself to be lovable, and loved. Here is the Ground of my Being, the explanation for my existence, here is true meaning, and here I want to stay.

Ignatius and his men were a new brand of religious. They were city men, at home in the expanding municipalities and city states of baroque Europe, and often working alone. The monks of the old Carthusian, Cistercian and Benedictine abbeys, on the other hand, were profoundly community men, and their religious houses were like fortresses of civilisation and stability when Europe was being torn apart, out in the country perhaps, but still focal points and places of employment for all the villages around. The third strand of prayer in the Church comes from yet a third direction, more stark and radical, and that is the desert. At the time of the Crusades, a group of men established themselves in a dry canyon in the Holy Land, on the slopes of Mount Carmel, in order to come close to God by lives of austerity and prayer. It was one of those windows in history which opened and then closed again. For a short time there was a Latin Kingdom of Jerusalem, which permitted westerners to take root in Israel, and these were Europeans who wanted to spend their lives in contemplation, to become hermits on the soil of Israel. Within a hundred years the Muslim conquest would force them out, but by that time their traditions were established. These early Carmelites were picking up, consciously or unconsciously, the prayer of Anthony and Pachomius in the Egyptian desert. The spiritual life was seen in stark terms: the Devil was on the prowl, and it was in the desert that the Christian had to stand up to temptations, suffer them, and by the grace of God defeat them. The conflict between Muslim and Crusader was mirrored by the inner conflict in the soul of the Carmelites. The weapons in the battle against evil were fasting, solitude, austerity and prolonged prayer. When circumstances forced them back to Europe, city life sapped their spiritual resources, and they underwent several reforms, some more successful than others. The most famous reform is that carried out by Teresa of Avila and John of the Cross in the sixteenth century.

Teresa's greatest contribution to Christian spirituality is found in her book *The Interior Castle*, which she wrote under obedience for the Sisters in her convent. She starts from the experienced fact that we spend much of our life fragmented by hundreds of different desires. The journey through the interior castle is a journey inwards through ourselves, into the depths of our own soul, and on this journey the multitude of our desires gradually gives way to one overpowering desire, for God. His mysterious presence is at the centre of us, in the castle keep, the fine point of our soul, and he draws us inwards. We progress deeper and deeper into the castle by faithfulness to prayer. As we progress we come to understand that holiness does not depend on our own efforts, but is a gift. We learn to abandon ourselves, renounce trust in our own strength, renounce even attachment to religious routines, and commit ourselves in total humility to this God who acts, and who always speaks first in the divine/human conversation. There will be tough patches on this journey, times even of torment, as we part company with so many of the props we previously considered indispensable. As we get closer to our goal, we may receive the gift of what Teresa calls 'infused prayer', a kind of prayer which is sheer gift of God and not engineered by ourselves, prayer which prays itself. The object of the journey is complete union of the soul with God. Teresa always makes the point that you judge the genuineness of your prayer in a very practical way. Am I playing my part in the community? Am I willing to be of service? Being far advanced in the spiritual life is never an excuse for contracting out. 'Let us desire and be occupied in prayer not for the sake of our enjoyment but so as to have the strength to serve . . .

Believe me, Mary and Martha must join together to show hospitality to the Lord.'* Teresa could not cope with Ignatian-style discursive prayer. She simply encouraged her nuns to focus on the person of Jesus: the humanity of Christ was always central to her.

John of the Cross wrote poems, many of them while he was imprisoned by the other Carmelites, the ones who did not want to be reformed. He underwent incredible suffering and at times his life was in danger, and yet simultaneously he produced the most sublime religious poetry ever written. Much of it was based on the Song of Songs in the Old Testament. Later he wrote commentaries to explain his poetry. The most famous ones are *The Spiritual Canticle, The Dark Night and the Ascent of Mount Carmel* and *The Living Flame of Love*. Indeed, these are more than commentaries – they are classics in their own right. The two images which dominate his writing are, first, that of the soul seeking union with God, the Beloved, in a way that is analogous to the sexual union of two lovers: the Song of Songs is, after all, superb love-poetry. Secondly, there is the image of the mountain to be climbed, again with the object of union with God at the top. The way to union with God is through self-denial: denial of the senses, a willingness to sacrifice everything that competes with our desire for God, and denial of our own religious satisfaction, our reliance on the consolations of religion, so that we place our trust uniquely in the Lord, just as Christ trusted his Father. It's a sheering away of the Frank Sinatra-type desire to 'do it my way'. John talks about the 'Dark Night of the Senses' and the 'Dark Night of the Spirit'. These are like tunnels through which we must expect to travel on our way to total union with God. We wave goodbye to any conceptual knowledge of God, and learn to find God in the *nada*, the nothing, the persevering contemplation of the cloak of darkness

---

* Teresa of Avila, *The Interior Castle, Classics of Western Spirituality* (Paulist Press)

in which God dwells. The darkness is in fact light, but to our feeble eyes it seems to be darkness. Incidentally, you find the same message in the fourteenth-century English classic, *The Cloud of Unknowing*.*

This chapter has offered only a pint-sized description of a lot of things, but you will have realised by now that these ways of praying all lead to the same place. If you are faithful to prayer, whatever your choice of method or tradition, you will gradually move away from the busy, the pictorial, the conceptual, and gradually your prayer will become simplified, as you lay hold more surely on God. You do it more with your heart than with your mind. The more you think about God, the more you realise that he is unknowable with the normal equipment he has given you. But so many possibilities remain. You can rest with him in that interior castle, person to person. You can stand before the cloud of unknowing and fire into it your darts, your arrows of faith, love and of longing. You can return again and again to the pages of Scripture and find in it the words which are your trampoline to prayer, because the Spirit who spoke through the prophets and the evangelists speaks also in your poor heart, and calls out, incessantly, on your behalf, 'Abba, Father.'

---

* *The Cloud of Unknowing* (Anon, fourteenth century), translated by Clifton Wolters (Penguin, 1961)

5

The Holy Spirit

Ronald Knox told the story in one of his published retreats about a small boy making his first confession. There was a lot of sucking of teeth and looking out of the window, before he risked everything and put all his cards on the table. 'Threw mud at buses and don't believe in the Holy Ghost,' he said. This chapter is not so much to investigate your feelings about the notorious 64 Rome bus, as to help you ask yourself the question 'Do I really believe in the Holy Spirit?' *Really*, that is, as opposed to notionally. The sequence for Pentecost says, '*Sine tuo numine, nihil est in homine*', which roughly translated is 'Without your aid nothing is in man.' Well, do I subscribe to that?

We are quietly sardonic about all kinds of religious enthusiasm, aren't we? And we have refined this attitude almost to an art form. We look at enthusiasm with a mixture of tolerance, amusement and slight irritation, rather as grandparents regard the antics of their grandchildren. 'Leave them alone – they'll soon grow out of it', that kind of thing. When we mock enthusiasm, what is the unspoken assumption? Surely it is that our way of being – institutional, placid and definitely non-enthusiastic – is the normal, grown-up way of being Church; it is, to use computer jargon, the default way of being a Christian. That's what we are implying. Anything else is transitory and suspect. The charismatic renewal, back in the seventies, excited all sorts of derision from people who didn't really understand it. On a slightly different tack, many parish priests would rather not have a mission preached in their parish. 'The results are never lasting, you know,' they say wisely. 'Within a few weeks everything is back to normal – and think of the expense! And all the preliminary effort!'

When the Holy Father opened the decade of evangelisation in 1990, not a few people could be heard saying, 'It's all been tried before. It's just another gimmick. There is nothing new under the sun.' When the regular *Ad Clerum** comes slipping through the presbytery door, and the PP sees 'Bishop's House' on the brown envelope, he sighs a lusty sigh into his cornflakes and says, 'I wonder what antics they want us to get up to now. Why can't these people leave us alone?' How easily we slip into a mode of being negative about all initiative. We fail to realise that what we implicitly promote is a vision of Church which is not only static but sterile. It is so easy to sit on the fence and carp. Clergy are good at it.

Clergy may be good at it, but it isn't the Gospel. Jesus Christ preached a word which was radical and profoundly disturbing: not disturbing like a parish mission where you can try to airbrush it out of your memory with the tail-light of the preacher, but disturbing in a way that simply won't go away. The words of the Sermon on the Mount hang over us; they are in the air all the time as a mute reproach but also a perpetual encouragement and invitation. 'I dare you,' says Jesus. 'I dare you to forgive your enemy and love him. I dare you to embrace poverty, and to give away your savings. I dare you to risk persecution in the cause of right. I dare you to be non-violent. I dare you to be chaste, not only in your behaviour, but also in your desires. I dare you to trust God your Father, instead of being riddled with anxiety.' A default lapse-back into placidity isn't even remotely on the agenda of Jesus. If it *was* anyone's agenda, it was that of the religious establishment of his time, who didn't want their boat rocked. They didn't want anyone daring them to do anything.

This is why Jesus has sent us the Spirit. It is precisely to stop us falling back into this default mode of placidity. What Jesus did and said was deeply upsetting. Revolution in religion started with his public life, and was meant to become endemic

* Bishop's circular

in the Church and in the world, really to the end of the world. What was he saying in Matthew 14 when he told Peter to come to him across the water? What was he saying in Mark 10 to the rich young man? What was he saying In Luke 5 when he told the disciples to put out into deep water? What was he saying in John 4 when he told them that the fields were white to the harvest? He was saying in each case and to all these people, 'Have a go. I know it's counter-cultural, but dare to have a go. I will send you the Spirit to look after you – you're in safe hands. But have a go.' He says to the people whose sins he forgives, 'Go now and sin no more.' Change is possible, he is saying: nobody has to be stuck, so long as they are courageous enough to have a go. When the parish priest organises a Penance Service before Christmas, and invites his colleagues to come and help with the confessions, does he hope in his heart of hearts that some sinners will repent, and alter their way of life, and never be the same again? Or has he quietly abandoned hope of this, and resigned himself to leading a flock where all the sheep are on a closed moral circle, and nothing changes, and the Easter Penance Service will be a carbon copy of the Christmas one? In other words, does he really believe in the Holy Spirit? Anyone starting to study the history of philosophy will find on the very first page that splendid pair Heraclitus and Democritus. Heraclitus thought that everything was in a state of constant flow. Democritus, who was the ancestor of today's atomic scientists, was convinced that nothing ever changed; it just got, so to speak, connected up differently. I think the abiding vice of the Catholic Church, if it has one, is a Democritus-type vice: that we have secretly lost hope that anything, or anyone, can be transformed.

'If we live by the Spirit, let us also be guided by the Spirit,' says Paul (Galatians 5:25). It is the Spirit, living within us, poured into our souls at baptism, who constantly nags away at us to take a chance in the name of the Gospel. The Spirit is God the Unexpected, God the Lightness of Touch, God who says, 'Don't get rooted in anything, don't get attached to any-thing, except me. Then you won't be heavy, and ponderous, and gloomy, and complicated. Then you'll be able to take on the big battalions at the bat of an eyelid, and not be fazed by them.' I love looking at Peter after Pentecost. What a changed man! See him in the Acts of the Apostles, doing a quick gallop through the Old Testament for the crowd in Jerusalem, completely forgetting that he is a backwoods fisherman from God-knows-where, and one of the lesser breed without the Law. 'Men of Judaea, make no mistake about this, but listen carefully to what I say' (Acts 2:14). What sublime nerve, to venture into the heart of theological orthodoxy, and talk like this off a soap-box. 'Oh, and by the way,' he says, 'we're not drunk, it's only nine o'clock in the morning.' Note the lightness of touch, the directness, the freshness of the way he speaks. Three thousand people ask for baptism that morning. He's at it again a chapter later in Acts, having cured the cripple at the Beautiful Gate: 'It is the name of Jesus which, through our faith in it, has brought back the strength of this man . . . Now you must repent and turn to God, that your sins may be wiped out' (Acts 3:16, 19). And he whacks in an airy reference to Moses and Abraham, just to prove to the crowd that all this is really kosher stuff, and not some weird oriental invention. A few verses later he is lecturing the High Priests, no less. He has been brought before them to be intimidated, but he takes the initiative. 'Then Peter, filled with the Holy Spirit, addressed them,' it says (Acts 4:8). Remember, this is the same Peter who, less than two months before, had lost his temper with the serving girl who said, 'Certainly you are also one of them, for your accent betrays you' (Matthew 26:73). The High Priests and the Sadducees jail the Apostles, and the angel immediately releases them, and here they are again before the Sanhedrin in chapter 5. 'We must obey God rather than any human authority,' they say (Acts 5:29). They are unsquashable and full of joy, even when they are imprisoned and threatened and flogged. They are living in another dimension, the dimension of the Spirit, and this makes their words irresistible and their courage total. Because of the fire and wind of Pentecost they have changed irreparably. Pope John Paul says this in *Dominum et Vivificantem*: 'Faith in its deepest essence is the openness of the human heart to the gift: to God's self-communication in the Holy Spirit.' Peter and his companions were open to the gift. Are you? The Pope again: 'Who will win? The one who welcomes the gift.'*

Why do you and I find this so hard to do? We have received the same Spirit as Peter, but somehow we don't manage to welcome it. We received the Spirit at our baptism, our confirmation, and some of us again at our ordination. Why doesn't it make any difference? Why do we behave as timorously and as cautiously as pagans? Why is our exposition of the Gospel often so leaden and so complicated? We pride ourselves on our fidelity to tradition, and we realise that the job of the magisterium is to pass on to succeeding generations the whole of the Catholic Faith, undiluted and undamaged. Those of us who are deacons and priests in the pulpit are, albeit humbly, a part of that magisterium. OK. But we do it with such effort and to so little effect. Let me give you what I think is the glimpse of a solution. You know that game 'Pass the parcel'. The players sit in a circle, and the music plays, and they pass from one to another a parcel with many wrappings. Every time the music stops, the person holding the parcel has to take a layer of wrapping off. The aim is not to be left holding the parcel when the music stops for the last time: that makes you the loser. So the trick is to pass the thing on very quickly, and unopened. Perhaps we regard the 'traditio fidei' in Catholicism in a similar light: no one can fault me if I pass on to you the truth I received from my own teachers, uninterfered with by me in any way, a closed parcel. But surely, if I am a Spirit-filled minister of God's word, what

---

* Encyclical of John Paul II, *Dominum et Vivificantem* (1986), paragraphs 51 and 55

I should be doing is opening the parcel, absorbing the contents, and then passing *myself* on to my people, a man informed and transformed by the Gospel and the Church's teaching. What made the Curé of Ars so convincing a preacher? Not the content of his sermons, which by all accounts was pretty dire, but the fact that he was utterly possessed and clearly lit up by the truth he was preaching. In other words, he lived in the Spirit. That was why he could not put a foot wrong. The same grace is on offer to you and me. Who will win? The one who welcomes the gift.

What is true of our preaching is true of our prayer. We get snarled up in systems and techniques. But the salient fact is that it is the Spirit, given to us as a free gift, who does the praying within us. Paul Murray, in a recent article, quoted a monk at Mont-les-Cats in France: 'Looking back, my impression is that for many, many years I was carrying prayer within my heart, but did not know it at the time. It was like a spring, but one covered with a stone. Then at a certain moment Jesus took the stone away. At that the spring began to flow, and has been flowing ever since.'* Many of us pray with Scripture. Well, the Spirit, given to us as a free gift, puts meaning into our reading of God's word. Listen to Michael Casey, the Australian Cistercian who is a superb authority on *Lectio Divina*: 'The Spirit is as active in the reading of the Bible as in its writing, because fundamentally the two activities are complementary facets of a single divine initiative . . . God not only speaks, but takes steps to ensure that what is said is also heard.'† It is almost like the image of someone playing tennis on both sides of the net at once: only divine ingenuity could devise this.

The Trinitarian pattern is: we pray to the Father, through the Son, in the Spirit. What does this mean? To oversimplify it,

---

* Paul Murray, article in *Spirituality*, vol. 6 (July/August 2000) (Dominican Publications, Dublin)
† Michael Casey, *Sacred Reading* (Liguori/Triumph Publications and Harper-Collins Religious, 1995)

it means that the Father and the Son are in front of us, but the Spirit is behind us and within us. He coaxes us on, triggering off our prayer, giving it meaning and sense, enabling us to do it. So much of the secret of prayer lies in letting him loose, if it is not irreverent to say this: positively inviting the Spirit to do what the Spirit knows how to do, and surrendering ourselves to the Spirit who delights to pray in us. Paul says to the Romans (8:26), 'The Spirit helps us in our weakness; for we do not know how to pray as we ought, but that very Spirit intercedes with sighs too deep for words.' So, our job is to go with the flow, and the flow is upwards. The Spirit gets inside the whole of God's creation, and most of all inside his human creation, and directs our gaze heavenwards, and enables creation to praise and love its Creator. 'The Spirit of the Lord fills the whole earth,' says the Book of Wisdom (1:7). We don't have to engineer this. It is a given.

St Leo the Great, writing on the work of the Holy Spirit, says this about Pentecost: 'From that day forth the trumpet of the preaching of the Gospel has sounded. From that day the rain of spiritual graces, the streams of blessings, have watered every desert, and the whole parched world: for the Spirit of God moved over the waters (Genesis 1:2) to renew the face of the earth, and the brightness of new life began to flash forth to scatter the old darkness, when in the splendour of those burning tongues, the shining word, the burning eloquence of the Lord was received; which holds within it both the power of making light, to give understanding, and the power of fire, to burn away all sin.'* People like Leo expected miracles, they expected conversions: they marvelled at them, but were not surprised at them, for they believed beyond doubt that the Spirit was at work in the Church and beyond it. Our problem is precisely this one of belief. We give notional assent to all the things we are supposed to believe, but then proceed to live as though they were not

---

* PL54, Serm. 75, Pentecost I, col. 400

true. We are rationalists by formation, all of us – no fault of ours – and the rationalist likes religion to stay safely private.

I suppose our lack of expectation is the one way in which we can stymie the work of the Spirit. For instance, we look at the different jobs a priest – or any Christian – might be asked to do, in his diocese or in the universal Church. Paul lists some of them in 1 Corinthians 12:28: 'God has appointed in the church first apostles, second prophets, third teachers; then deeds of power, then gifts of healing, forms of assistance, forms of leadership, various kinds of tongues.' Paul is listing these in the context of the Body of Christ, in which the Spirit of God binds us together. Paul sees the jobs that people get as the gift of the Spirit, not the outcome of some political process. We might add to the list: the marriage tribunal, the catechetical work of the diocese, the financial administration of the local Church, the fostering of vocations to the priesthood . . . even, dare I suggest it, the staffing of seminaries. If you are asked to do one of these things, will you see the power of the Spirit in that request, or will you reduce it to purely human terms, and say, 'Well, the Bishop really didn't have any choice.' Can you see what I mean? Relentlessly, we shorten the arm of the Lord, constrict his area of activity and power, abstract ourselves from his overarching plan, reduce everything to purely human agency. Basil the Great, on the other hand, says, 'Through his aid hearts are lifted up, the weak led by the hand, those going forward are perfected. Shining upon those who have been purified of every stain, he makes them spiritual in heart, through union with himself. For just as when the sunlight falls on clear transparent bodies, they too become resplendent, and begin to shine from another light within themselves, so the souls that contain the Spirit within them, become themselves spiritual, and their brightness shines forth on others.'* Ah, but do I want to become resplendent?

Who will win? The one who welcomes the gift.

---

* Basil the Great, *Liber de Spiritu Sancto*

6

Covenant

For any young person today, the notion of lifelong commitment may seem daunting. Whether they are thinking of getting married or becoming a priest, their reactions are predictable. 'What if it goes wrong?' 'Look at so-and-so, who only lasted a year in the priesthood, what if that happened to me?' 'How do I know what we shall be like in five years', ten years' time?'

In all these expressions of anxiety lurks this feeling: circumstances will decide the matter, circumstances are stronger than human determination, the human will cannot overcome circumstances. If I fall in love with a girl in the parish it will be like an express train, irresistible, there's nothing I can do about it. If I get bored with pastoral priesthood, it's irresistible, there's nothing I can do about it. If my faith gets weak, it's irresistible, there's nothing I can do about it. I shall be as helpless before these things as a tiny furry animal with the cobra's eyes upon it.

We know where a lot of this fear comes from. It comes from the chronic instability of social and family life. It comes from the many and sometimes notorious cases of men who have left the priesthood, some after a few months, some after many years. The received wisdom about fractured marriages says, 'It wasn't their fault – they just found they weren't in love any more.' Often a departing spouse will say to the abandoned partner, 'I have nothing against you, I just don't love you any more.' So there isn't an ascribable cause for the breakdown – it's just circumstances. A bit of bad luck, to be accepted fatalistically. As they say in Italian, *'Capita'* – 'It happens.' And you shrug your shoulders. Of a priest leaving the priesthood they say, 'He discovered that this was not his real vocation' or 'He realised that his vocation lay in another direction', as though he himself did not enter into this drama, it was all decided elsewhere; as if he had been duped when he spent six years in a seminary, did all that praying and discerning, and was solemnly called by the bishop. No, that wasn't a vocation after all, fancy that. In all these analyses of human inconstancy, the person who gives up is seen as the victim of circumstances, instead of being in some way the engineer and agent of his or her own destiny. I am not saying this in a reproachful or sarcastic way. I have enough inconstancy in my own track record to keep me very humble. It is simply a sidelong look at the way Western European society conducts itself and perceives itself. In a century of unparalleled human scientific achievement, we are less optimistic than we have ever been about the strength of the human character. We are all children of our age and civilisation, and we inhale the mores of our time along with the diesel fumes. *Capita.*

Against this background, to speak as we do about vocation to a life of service in one particular direction is countercultural, to say the least. How are we to approach it? It seems to me that Jesus, as the core of the spiritual life, is central to this question.

When Mass is celebrated the following words are said over the wine, that it is 'the blood of the new and everlasting covenant'. Here, I think, is the key. God always conducts his relationship with his people by deals, by contracts. In pre-Council moral theology we had to learn a lot about contracts, and they all had funny Latin names. '*Do ut facias*' was the contract where you paid a tradesman to come and do a job. '*Do ut des*' was what happened when you went shopping. '*Facio ut des*' was when you went to work in expectation of a wage . . . and so on. Well, God entered a contract with the children of Israel. 'Keep my Law, and I will give you a land flowing with milk and honey. Keep my Law, and I will change you from a crowd of nomadic warriors into a settled, pastoral, property-owning people. Keep my Law, and I will take away the precariousness of your lives and make you and your children prosperous.' The deal, the contract, was called a covenant. It was sealed by the slaughter of animals, whose blood was sprinkled partly on the altar and partly on the people, thus binding God and the Israelites together in a solemn life-and-death agreement. The covenant is mentioned over and over again in the Old Testament. As we know, the upshot was that the people, by and large, were not faithful to the covenant. They worshipped false gods, shaved bits off Sabbath observance, and treated one another unjustly. God promised, however, that he would always be faithful (Psalm 89:31-33): 'If they violate my statutes and do not keep my command-ments, then I will punish their transgression with the rod and their iniquity with scourges: but I will not remove from him my steadfast love, or be false to my faithfulness.'

We are children of the New Testament, which means New Covenant. The writing of inspired books may be over, but the covenant still runs, still holds. God has, in the most unex-pected way, been faithful. Just as the Jews were and are a covenanted people, so is the Church. The deal second time round is, however, wider and deeper. This time it is 'Attach yourself to my Son, believe in him, live by his Gospel, and I will give you not a piece of real-estate in Palestine but eternal life in my company.' And this time the covenant is sealed not by the blood of a bull but by the blood of Jesus. Had the covenant been a written document, it would have been signed with the blood of Christ. There is on earth nothing more solemn or serious than this. So, if you read the New Testament carefully, you realise how much faithfulness is once again in the air. God is constant in our regard, and we in our turn give our word to him. There are expectations on both sides. The first-born of the human race is Jesus, and he has demonstrated to us how to keep the covenant; he has modelled faithfulness for us. This is how human beings are to keep their side of the bargain, by persevering in spite of suffering, by loving even the unlovable, by embracing self-sacrifice, by being men and women of principle. The whole Church is built into Christ by baptism, so that in all Christian people Philippians 2:5 may come true: 'Let the same mind be in you that was in Christ Jesus.' And Jesus doesn't just model faithfulness; as we shall see later, he gives us the grace and power to be faithful men, faithful women.

The Testament itself, the covenant, the bargain, the deal still runs. As Christians we are supposed to live our lives in terms of that covenant. It should govern our behaviour. In a way it sits over us in judgement. We, as baptised people, are pledged to a certain kind of faithfulness. We don't have to make it up, it's in the document. Follow my Son, believe in him, live by his Gospel. That's our agenda. Now I, as a Catholic priest, am a leader of this covenanted people. My job is to help my flock be faithful, to model faithfulness for them, to be an example of faithfulness. My priesthood does not exist in a vacuum. It's not a private luxury or commodity. It only makes sense with reference to the people of whom I am a pastor, and of the fact that this people is committed to God in a special way. This commitment will see the people travelling through some lean times, just as the first one kept them wandering round the desert until Joshua finally led them home. Joshua, along with Moses, was expected to model patience and trust for the people. So am I. The lean times in our context are clear. We are in a cultural desert. We are despised and misunderstood by a civilisation which has veered into gross materialism. In Britain we are a minority (Catholics) within a minority (Christians) within a minority (believers), and the bulk of the population puts us all down as irrelevant. Some people even ascribe all the wars and tensions to us: Northern Ireland, Serbia and Croatia, the Taleban and the Twin Towers, the Nazis and the Jews, the Palestinians and the Israelis. None of these enormities would have taken place, they say, but for the poison of religious belief. Religious belief is of its nature intolerant, and gives a handle to people who are naturally violent. If we could purge the world of religious belief, we could all live together in harmony. Today's students are aware, more or less, that this is the atmosphere they have been living in since their childhood, an atmosphere which is becoming thicker as we speak, but they may not have reflected upon it. The big challenge is to be true to the Covenant. Constancy is not just a pious extra. I have given my word, and by the grace of God I will be true to it, and help my fellow-Christians to be faithful too.

A life of faithfulness to the new covenant must have Jesus at its centre. Without him we could not possibly attempt it. I talked earlier about Jesus 'modelling' faithfulness for us, and this is right. But it is far from being the whole story. Far from just being a good example, Jesus has a direct causal effect upon us. I love reading the preface of John's Gospel. 'All things came into being through him, and without him not one thing came into being. What has come into being in him was life, and the life was the light of all people. The light shines in the darkness, and the darkness did not overcome it.' Those words for 'life' and 'light' – 'zoe' and 'phos' – pack a terrific punch. Jesus brings us to life, like the dry bones in Ezekiel, like Lazarus stinking in his four-day tomb. Jesus floods us with light, with wisdom, with understanding, as he did the man born blind. If we stay close to him, he does these things for us. And if he does these things for us, then the darkness cannot overpower us. The paganness of Britain should convince us more and more of our radical need of him. We cannot coast along as some of our forefathers could do in a tribal religion. We need to be so close to Christ that his faithfulness and courage can swamp us, possess us, shine through us. 'God loved the world so much that he gave his only Son, so that everyone who believes in him may not be lost, but may have eternal life' (John 3:16). God's love is battering on our door and saying, 'Let me in, I want to give you eternal life.' God wants us to be faithful to the covenant.

I believe that concentration on the covenant, and on the

covenantal nature of our calling, whatever that calling may be, can be of great help to us. It is not a cold and demanding contract to which we are made signatories. On the contrary it is a promise and a guarantee of intimacy with a Lord who loves us to distraction. Listen to Hebrews, quoting Jeremiah. God is promising the new deal.

> I will put my laws into their minds,
> and write them on their hearts,
> and I will be their God,
> and they shall be my people . . .
> They shall all know me,
> from the least of them to the greatest.
> For I will be merciful toward their iniquities,
> and I will remember their sins no more.
> (Hebrews 8:10-12)

Each day commit yourself afresh, remembering this affectionate, heartfelt covenant:

> This is the cup of my blood,
> the blood of the new and everlasting covenant.
> It will be shed for you and for all
> so that sins may be forgiven.
> Do this in memory of me.

7

Experience of Jesus

I compare the life that awaits today's newly ordained priest with the life that awaited me, 43 years ago, when I emerged from the cocoon as a very insecure butterfly, and was appointed to be second curate in a parish. What I discovered was a cosy and tribal Anglo-Irish Church, full of customs elevated to the status of commandments. I was the child of a mixed marriage and had not been at a Catholic school, and was a bit short on the folklore. Seven years in Italy had not helped to keep me up to date with Catholic life as it was lived in Britain. I remember being called to the presbytery door and asked for a Mass card. 'Oh no,' I said, 'I don't think we have those in England.' The parishioner moved away cautiously, looking at me anxiously out of the corner of her eye. I can only guess what she told her family when she got home. Shortly afterwards it was Ash Wednesday, and I was nonplussed by the people who turned up after Mass with little twists of newspaper, rather like the salt packets you got in bags of crisps in those days: they wanted to take the ashes home and 'put them on the lodgers'. The parish priest had to reassure me about this, too. He was not there to reassure me about the funeral, when I forgot to put out the six unbleached candles round the coffin. I said airily, 'There's no time now – we'll do without', and was almost knocked down by the dramatic housekeeper, who came staggering out of the sacristy with a superhuman load of huge candlesticks, muttering darkly, 'Whoever heard of such a thing?' The Church of those days set its own agenda. It recited its immemorial devotional habits, and challenged new generations of Catholics and converts to live up to them. They were boom years, with plenty of converts and plenty of ordinations. We lived life in a very small contained orbit, summed up and described every week by the Catholic press, which was largely uncritical and triumphalist: caricatured by the spoof headline, 'Catholic cow has Catholic calf.' We refought the battles of the Reformation, licked our wounds and prayed for the Conversion of England – by which we meant the unravelling of Protestantism. Beyond this we could not see very far. The England of those days was still nominally Christian, with official allegiance to Christian standards of morality. Immigration was in its infancy. Pluralism had not even been thought of.

Today's situation could not be more starkly different. There is no cosy tribal Anglo-Irish Church: it has evaporated. The main body of society no longer pays lip-service to Christian belief or morality. Not to say that it has discovered an alternative belief or morality – it has simply lurched sideways into agnosticism, amorality and the public pillory. Reversing the Reformation would not solve the problem. No religion commands respect, and professional religious people command it even less. We Catholics no longer perceive the reformed Churches as the enemy. We are, instead, face to face with a ruthlessly commercial civilisation which values only what is useful and profitable. The media treat religion as a minority sport, like morris dancing or clay pigeon shooting, a pastime for the eccentric. Very few people go to any church. The Catholic body has shrunk through lapsation. Our Catholic newspapers have become peevish and sectional. There are fewer priests than before, their average age is increasing, and the supply of vocations has dwindled to a tiny trickle. We are closing and merging parishes, and talking of closing seminaries. The bright side is that the fields are white to the harvest as never before. People have become aware that modern TV/ technological society does not satisfy the cravings of the heart.

The great challenge now, rightly highlighted by the Pope, is evangelisation. Europe, and in particular Britain, needs to be re-evangelised. It is harder to re-evangelise than to evangelise because the language has all been used up. The public already knows the vocabulary, or thinks it does, and has rejected it. How do we find an idiom which will register with post-Christian people?

The nearest parallel I can find is that of the early Church. The early Church had to cope with defections, and internal arguments, as well as the disdain of society at large. There were times when you would not have given 10 pence for its survival: it looked doomed, from within and without. The Decree of the Senate in AD 35 refers to Christianity as '*strana et illicita*' (strange and illegal). Tacitus calls it '*exitialis*' (lethal). A few decades later the historian Suetonius labels the Christian Faith as '*nova et malefica*' (new and pernicious). These condemnations were accompanied by periodic ethnic cleansing: the Romans were apprehensive of anything nonconformist – i.e. unwillingness to sacrifice to the Emperor. The killings under Nero, Domitian, Marcus Aurelius, Decius, Valerian and Diocletian are legendary. What kept Christianity afloat, and what assured its ultimate health and growth, was the small number of men and women whose personal faith in Jesus was unshakeable. Pope John Paul, speaking of the Catacombs in Rome, says, 'We can, so to speak, touch with our hands the faith which animated the ancient Christian community.' It was faith in Jesus risen and ascended, Jesus who would come again to gather together the elect. For his sake it was worth undergoing all kinds of privations and persecutions. Indeed, the privations and persecutions were allowed for in Scripture; they were to be expected. 'For him I have accepted the loss of everything, and I look on everything as so much rubbish if only I can have Christ and be given a place in him . . . All I want is to know Christ and the power of his resurrection and to share his sufferings by reproducing the pattern of his death' (Philippians 3:8-10). Christianity, in spite of all the dangers it carried with it, was a powerfully attractive religion at the time of the early Church.

Here is Ignatius writing to the Romans at the start of the second century: 'Him I seek, who died for us: Him I desire, who rose again for our sake . . . If anyone has Him within himself, let him consider what I desire, and let him have sympathy with me.' Familiar words, but remarkable still: the passion and death of Christ had power to motivate people in the most amazing way. He continued, after the Ascension, to be a living force.

Listen to Pliny's complaint in his tenth Letter, during Trajan's reign: 'Many people of every age and class and of both sexes are called for trial, and will continue to be called. And it's not only in the cities. The villages and the countryside are also soaked by the contagion of this superstition.' Pliny called the new religion *'prava et immodica'* – depraved and unbridled – although he could not find fault with the actual practices of Christians.

And 80 years later, Tertullian: 'People complain that the town is full of Christianity, that there are Christians in the countryside, in the market towns, in every block of flats there are Christians. People of every age, sex, condition and social rank are being converted to this name: and this is officially regretted as though it were a public misfortune.'* And he spells out the reason for the faith and the courage of Christians: 'With nothing more than his word he [Jesus] cast out devils from the bodies of men, he gave back sight to the blind, he healed lepers, he made the paralytics walk, and still with his word he even brought the dead back to life. The very elements were compelled to obey him. Dominating storms, and walking on the waters of the sea, he showed that he was that Son forecast by God, born for the salvation of men, the original and firstborn Word of God, inseparably accompanied by power and reason, and borne along by the Spirit.' Tertullian goes on to describe the resurrection: 'On the third day the earth was suddenly shaken, and the great stone which enclosed the sepulchre was rolled away, the guards scattered in terror . . .' He retails the account from Matthew's Gospel, of the money

---

* Apol., I, 6

paid to the soldiers by the High Priest, to assert that the Apostles had stolen the body, and he says that the Risen Christ did not appear to the crowds and dispel this rumour because he didn't want Christian faith to be cheap – *'non mediocri praemio destinata'*; it was meant to be tough. And then he describes the 40 days, and the Ascension. He goes on, 'His disciples, scattered throughout the world as their divine Master had commanded, and obeying his word, suffered grievous persecutions at the hands of the Jews, and ultimately, with faith in the truth, sowed Rome with their Christian blood during the cruel reign of Nero.'* For us in the twenty-first century there are no surprises here, although it is good to know that at the start of the third century Christians were articulating their faith substantially as we articulate ours. What makes Tertullian worth quoting is that this simple statement of faith attracted innumerable converts, at high risk of torture and death. The limpid truth of the Gospel was utterly convincing. At the turn of the third century, the person of Jesus was irresistible.

What made, and makes, the person of Jesus irresistible is not sweet reason, or apologetic argument. It is the gift of the Spirit, isn't it? Christ, ascended into heaven, sends the Spirit to re-convert the Apostles and set the whole Church in motion. Pentecost. Without the Spirit the whole operation would have been stillborn. The Church comes to life in high drama, and continues to spread dramatically. The Acts of the Apostles make this clear. The Apostles speak, more or less eloquently, and then the Spirit strikes, affecting not only the preachers but the listeners too. The accounts of the life, death and resurrection of Jesus would not in themselves have been sufficient to make people alter their lives and, indeed, risk them. No account would. Some other agency had to intervene, and we call that agency the Holy Spirit. It is the Holy Spirit who elicits that wholehearted 'Yes' to the preaching of

* Apol., XXI, 25

the Gospel, today as in apostolic times. Experience of the living God means being seized, in some way, by the Spirit. Paul says in Philippians (3:12), 'I am still running, trying to capture the prize for which Christ Jesus captured me.' The word he uses for 'captured' is very forceful: it has overtones of 'overcome' or 'seized'. If you listen to the experience of people who come to the RCIA, you realise that the Spirit is still at work, and often in the most unlikely people, people like Saul of Tarsus, only in the twenty-first century. That's where modern-day prophets come from. Our mistake is not to believe this.

Our other mistake is not to believe this about ourselves. When we have the leisure to survey the path which has led us to where we are, a path which includes the parents God gave us, the schools we went to, the sins we committed, the people who had most influence on us, the efforts we made, our failures, our successes, our deep sorrows, our moments of happiness and discovery . . . have we the courage to say that yes, the finger of God is clearly detectable – here, and here, and here? Evangelicals have stolen the language of 'When did you first accept Christ as your personal Lord and Saviour?' I remember them waylaying South American language students in Cambridge, and taking them away to a Christian Tea, and asking them, 'When, on what day, did you become a Christian?' and the South Americans answering, in all simplicity, 'I am not a Christian, I am a Catholic.' The evangelicals would say, 'In that case, you are going to hell.' Tidying up the mess which resulted from this misunderstanding, and drying the tears of beautiful Colombian girls with very faulty English, caused me to think about this question in some depth.

It is true that many Catholics grow up with the Faith unconsciously, and do not notice the transitions, rather as a baby is weaned from mother's milk on to more solid stuff without paying much attention. If their family is strongly Catholic they grow up with good habits of practice and prayer, and mature in their Catholicism without abrupt moments of revelation. However, even for such lucky people, and there are fewer and fewer of them these days, there does come an occasion, I'm sure of this, when they get a second wind, a new realisation, an ability to focus on God and recognise him in a new way. It isn't something you can engineer: God himself is the architect of it, and he picks his '*kairos*', his time. It may come from exposure to an inspiring figure, like a university chaplain. It may come from a group experience, like the Charismatic Renewal. It may come from membership of one of the new 'movements' in the Church. It may come from taking handicapped kids to Lourdes. It often has a profound and lasting effect.

For others, and they are probably the majority, a theoretical belonging to the Catholic Church has not prevented them from floating away from the Faith, intellectually and morally, and what they experience later is a full-blown conversion. Again, it is God who picks the moment and the means. What is essential is for us to be able to recognise these divine interventions, and to name them. A large part of evangelisation is being willing to talk about them. Men of my generation were taught to distrust experience, to suspect it of being pure emotion or of having some purely physical explanation. In any case, to talk about yourself was incredibly big-headed. Our approach to Catholicism was dreadfully rationalistic. We instructed converts, not in the overwhelming goodness of God, but in the correctness of our arguments. It was a cold-blooded business. We Catholics have to rediscover the idiom of the divine call which comes one-third of the way or half-way through life. God does not just sit still and have statements made about him. He takes the initiative in his relationship with us.

And this initiative is today what it was 2000 years ago. It is the gift of Jesus. Teresa of Avila used to tell her sisters that the humanity of Christ was a sure and secure way to God. As for them, so for us. The person of Our Lord is held out to us by the Father so that we may know, appreciate and love him

– so that we may actually have someone to know, appreciate and love – and be aware that he knows, appreciates and loves us. The Risen Christ is for now, not for history. We are not dwelling in the grey and chilly uplands of theory, where people fence with theological opinions as though with rapiers. We are invited to something much warmer: a real and personal experience of Jesus.

8

In Praise of the Collective

One of the horrors of Communism at its height was its ruthless subjection of the individual to the collective. My mother used to frighten me as a small boy with tales of Soviet experiments, in which no child had an individual mother or father but all the children belonged to the commune, and were looked after by appointed child-minders. The Soviet agricultural reforms of the 1930s cost hundreds of thousands of lives because the process of dismantling private homesteads was dreadfully maladministered. Millions of people, especially in the Ukraine, collapsed into famine. As an economic system, Communism manifestly failed. Margaret Thatcher lost no occasion of pointing this out. On a lighter note, Peter Ustinov used to sing a spoof Russian song called, I think, 'The lament of the collective farmer whose tractor has betrayed him'. The ethos of Britain, and indeed of Europe, over the last 30 years has been severely individualistic: look after yourself and your family. 'Society' as such is seen as something much more nebulous, too shifting a sand on which to build anything. So to call this chapter 'In Praise of the Collective' is to fly in the teeth of a prevailing wind. But we are disciples of Jesus, and as such we belong to his Church, because that is what he wants of his disciples. And this involves a counter-cultural mentality. Let's see.

I remember an old lady I used to visit years ago. Eva, her name was. Eva was 88 in 1961, so she was born in 1873: very much a Victorian, with a Victorian forthrightness and turn of phrase. She was a bit like Miss Havisham in *David Copperfield*. She would sit in a high-backed chair, with her lively, penetrating eyes piercing everything and everybody, wrap herself in her shawl and deliver herself of sharp Olympian judgements. At some stage she had been converted to Catholicism, but in what Cardinal Hume was later to call an 'à la carte' fashion. 'I believe in God,' she would say in a high, clear voice, 'but I can't be doing with the Church.' Somewhere along the line she had been offended – by something a Pope had written, or a bishop had said, or a priest had done. She had washed her hands of the Church, believing she could see over its head, so to speak, and have a direct line to God.

How important it is for us to realise that the Church, with all its spots and wrinkles, is God's will and God's project and God's darling and the apple of God's eye. This in spite of the fact that sometimes the Church in her human dimension is quite exasperating, scandalous and disappointing. When we work for the spiritual good of the Church, we work for God. God has always dealt with us collectively in the first place, individually in the second place. It's his style. Read the Old Testament, and you will appreciate how God treats the whole Hebrew people as what Canon Law calls a moral person, with group responsibility for its behaviour. 'O house of Jacob, come, let us walk in the light of the Lord!' (Isaiah 2:5) And in the Reproaches for Good Friday: 'My people, what have I done to you? How have I offended you? Answer me.' He even has a name for the people; he calls it 'Israel', and refers to it as 'he' and 'him'. Hosea 11:1: 'When Israel was a child, I loved him, and out of Egypt I called my son.' There is no clear distinction between the fate of the king and the fate of the people. Remember the episode in 2 Samuel 24 when David counts the inhabitants of Israel and Judah, and God is angry, and sends a pestilence on the land which kills seventy thousand. Our sense of justice, if we're not careful, is outraged by this. 'It wasn't the people's fault,' we say, because we are deeply imbued with the individualism of our time. Indeed, God's ways are not ours, and nor are his thoughts. In his eyes the people as a whole is party to the covenant. The people as a whole is unfaithful to the covenant. The people as a whole goes into exile. The people stands or falls together. We write this approach off, perhaps, as belonging to the Old Testament. Now, we say, we know better. But does not the New Testament, too, obstinately favour the collective?

At Pentecost the Spirit came to found the Church. The Spirit came not primarily as a personal gift to Peter, Andrew, James and John, to make them intelligent and brave, but for the sake of the Church. 1 Corinthians 12:13 says, succinctly, 'For in the one Spirit we were all baptised into one body.' *Lumen Gentium* no. 5 says, 'Really sharing in the body of the Lord in the breaking of the eucharistic bread, we are taken up into communion with him and with one another.' And this paragraph quotes Corinthians again (1 Corinthians 10:17): 'Because the bread is one, we, though many, are one body, all of us who partake of the one bread.' We are Body. We are Communion. The point bears labouring. It is so easy for us to grow up with a highly personal perception of what religion is. To see it as a source of comfort for myself. To see it above all as a means by which I may save my soul. To see the main weight of religious activity as intensely private: my task is to avoid polluting my soul with grave sin, my task is to carry out my religious duties, my task is to make myself virtuous and above reproach, so that when I die I may go to heaven. Of course there is truth in these formulations, but against them you have to set the words of the Gospel: 'For whoever wants to save his life will lose it; and whoever loses his life for my sake, he will save it' (Luke 9:24). This paradox of Jesus means, in effect, that you save your soul by committing yourself hook, line and sinker to God and your neighbour, rather than by burnishing your own image. True religion draws you into self-forgetful unselfishness, not introspection. Our personal salvation is at the same time a primary goal and a side effect. Only Jesus could unite such apparent opposites. Thus it is that I achieve holiness by my insertion in the Church through baptism and the Eucharist, and by my commitment to the Church in my daily life. The Church feeds me with life. By being plugged into the Church, by living her sacramental life, I become heir to all the blessings God has promised his people. In return I feed the Church with my loyalty, my energy and my love.

Commitment to the Church takes concrete forms. For most Catholics it means commitment to their parish. This particular group of people, with its pastor, has been given to me to love. I may have reservations about the way they conduct their affairs. They may sing like corncrakes and park their cars most selfishly. But if I am a wise disciple of Christ, I will realise that my vocation is to throw my lot in with them, and not look for more congenial surroundings. To say, 'I go to the neighbouring church, because the times are convenient for me, because the preaching is better, because I prefer the music' is to miss the point. It is to bring the ideology of the supermarket into the parish: the unspoken axiom that we have a fundamental right to choice in everything, and that we shop around for what we like best. Some years ago a friend of mine, a German missionary in the Mato Grosso, one of the most remote parts of Brazil, was on a visit to New York. It was a Saturday night, and the priest with whom he was staying (and who told me the story) took him down the road to the food mall to do some weekend shopping. When he entered the store, and looked around, the missionary lost his head, began to shout, and had to be hustled out again at top speed. What had caused this rush of blood to the head? It was the amount of choice on the shelves. He found it mind-blowingly scandalous that the ordinary citizens of the US, in an ordinary suburb, could pick between six kinds of cornflakes and 12 brands of peanut butter and 18 varieties of dogfood while his own parishioners were struggling to stay alive. He had forgotten just how much Europe and North America had bought into the ideology of choice. The same ideology afflicts the Church. People shop around. If, however, you don't shop around, loyalty to your own parish will offer you the chance, sooner or later, to make things better. This is the group of believers with whom the Lord wants you to celebrate the Eucharist. If you don't stick with your parish, but hunt for aesthetic satisfaction elsewhere, you will never have that chance to make things better. Your exercise of choice will have been a negative thing.

What is true of the parish is true of the diocese. Even more true, because the diocese is not just an administrative slice of the Catholic Church but the whole mystery of the Church in miniature. In *Christifideles Laici*, John Paul II says, 'The particular Church [diocese] does not come about from a kind of fragmentation of the universal Church . . . The universal Church exists and is manifested in the particular Churches.'* If, as it says in Ephesians (5:25), Christ delivered himself up to make the Church holy, then he delivered himself up to make your diocese holy. If, as Paul says in 1 Corinthians (3:9) and Peter says in his first letter (2:7), the Church is the building of God, with Jesus himself as the cornerstone, then your diocese is the building of God, with Jesus as the cornerstone. Vatican II takes the text from Apocalypse 21 about the new Jerusalem and applies it. Let's just look at it now, but remembering that 'the new Jerusalem' dreamed of in this vision is not just the universal Church, but equally your diocese. You may have a pretty prosaic view of your diocese, with its personalities who could be a touch unimaginative, and an administrative machine which is, who knows, a bit ponderous and pedestrian? Nevertheless it is our belief that here, 'shining through our human weakness' as the Preface says, the full mystery of the Church is present.

> Then I saw a new heaven and a new earth;
> for the first heaven and the first earth had passed away,
> and the sea was no more.
> And I saw the holy city, the new Jerusalem, coming down
> out of heaven from God,

---

* Apostolic Exhortation of John Paul II, *Christifideles Laici* (1988), paragraph 25

prepared as a bride adorned for her husband.
And I heard a loud voice from the throne saying,
'See, the home of God is among mortals.
He will dwell with them as their God;
they will be his peoples, and God himself
will be with them;
he will wipe every tear from their eyes.
Death will be no more; mourning and crying and pain
will be no more,
for the first things have passed away.'
And the one who was seated on the throne said,
'See, I am making all things new.'

Apocalypse 21:1-5

There are many ways of exercising your Catholic faith. Pope John Paul has pointed out the great capacity of '*I Movimenti*' – the movements – to revitalise and re-evangelise the Church. But he has also pointed out that this must not be done to the prejudice of diocese and parish. Diocese and parish are Premier League when we are deciding where to put the lion's share of our loyalty and energy. It is through diocese and parish that 99 per cent of the Catholic faithful around the world have access to the word of God, the Eucharist and the sacraments. If we are serious Catholics we will not walk away from diocese and parish, but put our back into making them what they should be. Now, if this is true of laymen and laywomen, it has to be even more true of clergy, priests or priests-to-be. You do come across priests who turn their back on the diocese, maybe because of enthusiasm for a particular movement, maybe because of a row with the bishop, maybe out of a distaste for the other clergy of their neighbourhood. I recall one man who made the annual announcement to his parishioners, when money was needed for the old and infirm brethren, 'The second collection today is for priests who are sick of the diocese.' A joke, of course. The diocese deserves our enthusiasm, our energy, our loyalty. By giving these we don't just gratify the bishop: we build up the Body of Christ.

In this chapter I have tried not to use the word 'community'. It's a personal thing. I feel that both in the Church context and in others, the word is over-used. Ever since I was a boy people have talked about 'the criminal community' as if all the burglars in the world belonged to a club, which had monthly meetings, elected its own chairman and treasurer, and had an annual outing to the seaside. People who do similar things do not necessarily belong to a community at all. 'Community' in the ecclesial sense has a specialised meaning, and is best applied to religious orders. For a religious, the welcome and charity shown to other members of the household is not just something highly desirable, it is the very texture of Christian living, it is the stuff of vocation; it is not just something that underpins the job, it is itself the job. In a religious house, people have contracted for community, they have actively sought it; we who don't belong to religious orders do not have a direct vocation to on-the-spot community. What we do have, however, is an urgent summons by God to practise charity to all members of the household of the faith. That text in Galatians 6:10 is very revealing. Here it is in the New Jerusalem version.

> So then, as long as we have the opportunity
> let all our actions be for the good of everybody,
> and especially of those who belong to the household of
> the faith.

The Greek word for the people in the household is '*oikeious*' which really means family members, relatives, insiders, as opposed to '*paroikous*' who are the strangers and the temporary lodgers. Paul is saying to the Galatian Christians, 'You must care for everyone you meet, but have a special solicitude for your fellow-Christians.' They are your household. We have been given to one another to love, that's what it comes to.

I can't live the Christian life authentically without belonging.

9

Feeding the People

Do you remember the occasion when Jesus and the disciples are really tired, and Jesus suggests a day off? 'Let's go to a quiet place where we can be alone.' So they set off in the boat, cross the lake, and incautiously put in to shore in a spot where they naively think they will be left to themselves. We know what happens. The crowd have tracked him from the bank, and they've guessed where he's going, and they have hurried ahead and forestalled him, and there they all are on the beach. Matthew 9:36 describes Our Lord's response (this is the Jerusalem translation): 'And when he saw the crowds he felt sorry for them because they were harassed and dejected, like sheep without a shepherd.' So this is a man with a heart. Even when he is trying desperately to find some repose, he cannot prevent this instinctive movement of concern, of sympathy, for people who are harassed and dejected. He could see it in their faces. An older version says 'he had compassion on the multitude'. People like this have a slightly helpless, vacant, but above all appealing look. It was a look Our Lord could not resist. Mark 6:34 says, 'He set himself to teach them at some length.'

In Mark's Gospel this episode is immediately followed by the feeding of the five thousand. It must have been really 'at some length' that he spoke, because, says Mark, 'by now it was getting very late'. We witness again the compassion of Jesus for ordinary people, people whom he did not know by name, people in large numbers. In the second miracle of the loaves in Matthew (15:32) we hear Our Lord saying, 'I feel sorry for all these people; they have been with me for three days now and have nothing to eat. I do not want to send them off hungry, they might collapse on the way.' This is not the language of a man who is just an enthusiast for a cause – it is the language of a man who has a great affection and tenderness for people, for people in large numbers, for what used to be called the Great Unwashed. So what does he do? He feeds them, feeds them so well that the leftovers are far in excess of the loaves and fishes he started with.

There is a powerful truth here, if we have ears to hear. When we go to Mass, when we celebrate Mass, what is going on? Why, the people are being taught. (I don't mean this in a patronising way, as if 'the people' were some lower form of life. I too am people. I too need teaching.) They are being taught at some length, what with the Old and New Testament readings, the responsorial psalm, the Gospel and the homily. And then they are being fed. They are fed with the bread of angels, fed with the food of eternal life. The compassion which Jesus has for ordinary people, which he showed for ordinary people in the Gospel, is being expressed in our churches, Sunday by Sunday. He feeds us with his word and his body. And he does it with great affection. He doesn't want us to collapse on the way. Some of the people do not listen when the Scriptures are read, or do not understand them; some of the people, technically speaking, should not be coming to communion. It does not occur to them to ask – they come to the altar in good faith – and the priest is not equipped with second sight. The compassion of Jesus reaches through to those people as well. There is always an unevenness in large groups of people, and he knew this when he started preaching in Galilee, and he went out to meet them all with much love, with unconditional love. This unconditional love is not just an element in the Gospel – it *is* the Gospel. God's unconditional love for us is the Good News: there is no better news.

When a man takes the road to the priesthood he becomes a lector and an acolyte. By these ministries the Church makes explicit the various elements which are present in priesthood.

Priesthood is a ministry of word, and a ministry of sacrament. These skills are learned one by one, but it is only in priestly ordination that they will be brought together – with the ministry of service contained in the diaconate – into a harmonious whole. Meanwhile, it is not a bloodless series of performances, reading the scriptures and distributing communion. It is a loving, nourishing service rendered to the people whom the Lord loves. When a woman loves her child she feeds it: there is no more loving thing she can do. (Some women even over-feed their children and make them too fat, because they are so anxious to express their affection.) It should be impossible for me to proclaim the Old and New Testaments, or to distribute communion to a congregation, without sharing in that movement of the heart which is so characteristic of Jesus – 'he had compassion on the multitude'. I have nothing better than this to put before them: word and sacrament, with compassion. If this is true of priests, it is true of readers and eucharistic ministers as well.

My desire for the people is that they should grow, both individually and as a Church. The state of people's souls, and the state of the Church at large, are things that matter to me. Priest or not, I cannot remain indifferent to them. Every lapse from grace, every loss of faith, every scandal hurts me. Every conversion, every repentance, every vocation answered, every shared experience of faith delights me. I develop what the Pope in *Pastores Dabo Vobis** calls a '"pastoral charity", whose essential content is "the gift of self" . . .', a concern for the flock of God. My concern is not patronising or disdainful, because I know my own sinfulness and weakness. But it is still the concern of a shepherd, because through no merit of mine the Lord has put into my hands the resources with which to help people, and I want to use these resources to maximum advantage. Occasionally you come across priests

---

* Apostolic Exhortation of John Paul II, *Pastores Dabo Vobis* (1992), paragraph 23

69

who are quite hard-hearted, and dismissive of the ordinary folk in their parishes. We should take care never to get like that. Our ministry is of its nature a tender one. See how first-time parents talk to their baby children, long before the children can answer. They give them words to assemble when the time comes, they give them the building-blocks of speech. Spiritually, we do this when we share the scriptures, even with quite uneducated audiences. That's why it is so important to read well, audibly, and with expression. Then watch how the first-time parents feed their children, long past the milk stage, introducing them slowly to solid food, but doing so with infinite patience and care. All that cajoling with teaspoons, all that gravy scattered to the four winds, all those sonorous burps. To eat well is a science which we learned when we were little, and by now take for granted. We acquired it because there were grown-ups who loved us, and who were prepared to spend hours feeding us. That same solicitude and warmth should be present when we give communion to a congregation of people. This is not an automatic function, but a deeply personal one.

The same thing applies, clearly, when, as priest, deacon or eucharistic minister, we take communion to the sick and the housebound. They are not always, it must be admitted, the most responsive of human characters. Every priest can tell hospital stories. 'Would you like me to bring you Holy Communion in the morning?' 'If you like.' Or another reply might be, 'If it does me no good it'll do me no harm.' I remember one old lady who wanted communion at home, but very much on her terms: if you arrived while they were saying the Rosary on Vatican Radio, you got an earful. I remember in my first appointment taking communion several times to another old lady who seemed to me perfectly healthy. I asked my predecessor about it. 'Oh yes,' he said, 'she has simply developed a liking for communion at home.' Another one, in a village some way from the church, let slip that she went for rides on her bicycle, although she always jumped into bed when I rang the doorbell. When you inherit a communion round, there will be some characters on it about whose faith you are very doubtful, like the old man who is always consuming a pint of stout, smoking a disgusting pipe and reading *The Sun* when you arrive, and who is incapable of clearing even the tiniest flat space on which you can put your crucifix, candles and corporal: you end up giving him the Lord straight from the pyx round your neck. All these eccentricities are part of illness and old age. They may, objectively, be incorrect. They are, however, thoroughly human, and Jesus had a disarming delight in things – and people – who were thoroughly human. You have to be slow to judge and quick to smile, and hang on like mad to your sense of humour. I remember being so distracted on one occasion that I cycled about four miles into the country before realising that I had forgotten to take the Blessed Sacrament from the tabernacle. These are his people, the sheep of his flock. Loving them is more important than licking them into shape. When you set out on your monthly round, remind yourself that however things work out on the ground, you are doing the supreme service to people who really matter. And if you train others for this task, make sure you do a session on this, on the motivation and the spirit with which we embark on it. Being a eucharistic minister is not a power-trip or a prestige-symbol; quite the reverse.

How lucky we are to have the Eucharist to give, and to have such a clearly defined belief about it. Imagine what life would be like in the Church if we were non-sacramental Christians, depending entirely on the Bible, and hanging grimly on to some impossibly fundamentalist interpretation of it. People live their religion by action as much as by word. There is a gesture of huge significance in giving your brother or your sister the Bread of Life, even if nothing is said. The tiny host is deceptively simple and unassuming, yet it is the centre of our reverence and our adoration: and this, most precious of all imaginable gifts, I bring you because I care about you, and to show you that God cares about you. At the end of the Second World War there were many stories about the Eucharist in occupied Europe. I knew a Polish priest who had been in Dachau. My recollections of what he said are confused now, but I think he told me that he had celebrated Mass (from memory) lying on his side under the bed in the dormitory block, with a few scraps of bread and a tiny quantity of wine that had been smuggled in. He was able to give communion to quite a number of people, right under the noses of the guards. Another account described how a young deacon was arrested and sent to a concentration camp. He contracted TB, and clearly did not have long to live. The priests in the camp wanted to see him ordained a priest, and they set about praying for a solution. Sure enough, the Germans arrested a French bishop and put him in the camp, and he agreed to do the ordination. The whole thing was conducted secretly. The young man offered Mass just once, in secret. When the Americans arrived and liberated the prisoners, the new priest went straight to hospital and he died. In Catholic terms, his life was a resounding success. It was a success in the terms of what matters most.

What matters most is that the people should be fed.

10

Freedom

The story is told of a Marxist orator on his soapbox at Speakers'
Corner in London. He was holding forth to a small group of
admirers. Pointing vaguely in the direction of Park Lane he
said, 'When the Day of Freedom comes, comrades, you will
be riding in those Rolls Royces, and you will be living in
those penthouse flats.' A little man at the back interrupted
him. 'Excuse me,' he said, 'but I get carsick in Rolls Royces,
and I get vertigo at the top of buildings.' The orator fixed
him with a stony glare and said, 'Comrade, when the Day of
Freedom comes, you will do what you are bloody well told.'

What is freedom, and how important is it? People often
think that the opposite of freedom is obedience. The truly free
spirit, they say, owes obedience to nobody. He does his own
thing. He is like Clint Eastwood, riding into town, polishing
off the corrupt sheriff single-handed, and riding out again,
following his individual and lonely star, conforming to no
one else's rules. This is the iconography of the Wild West. It
doesn't have much to do with the Gospel. It is responsible, I
suspect, for a lot of broken marriages: 'I couldn't bear to be
tied down. I had to break away and be my own self.' At root,
that's a pretty selfish idea of freedom.

The worst kind of old-fashioned novice masters (and novice
mistresses) saw it as their job to break the spirit of the novices,
to drain out of them any hint of independence or initiative, so
that they would be immediately and unthinkingly responsive
to the commands of their superiors. The thinking behind this
went as follows. Life is a series of crunches, of staccato stand-up
fights between the rebellious human will and the law of God
and the Church. The only way to make us holy is to crush the

old Adam (and the old Eve) by teaching us our obligations, and by indicating the punishment that will follow if we break the rules. Thus, slowly and painfully, we are trained to subject ourselves to the will of God, expressed in the commands of those set over us. Obedience is the name of the game. Each of those stand-up battles of human will versus divine law must be won by God. We turn our back on freedom in the name of obedience. Hence those horror stories about novices being told to plant cabbages upside down, or pay the butcher's bill with bags of pennies, or wash the stairs from the bottom up instead of from the top down. I remember an old bishop saying, many moons ago, 'What the Church demands of her priests, above all, is obedience.' Ours not to reason why, ours but to do and die, into the valley of death rode the six hundred.

That's a pretty bleak model of spirituality – and a pretty arid kind of moral theology. I think we can do better than that. You see, you were born with a measure of autonomy and self-determination which, quite simply, goes with being a human being. No one has the right to deprive you of that. No one has the right to turn you into a set of knee-jerk responses, or some kind of a puppet, or a cog in someone else's machine. If God had wanted you to be like that he would not have made you intelligent. From the first moment of existence you have had the gift of free will, of choice. This is the finest element in your character, not something sinister and dangerous. You did not receive it simply in order to give it away. It is significant that Jesus was entirely obedient to the will of his Father, but he was a supremely free man.

Hot on the heels of the gift of free will, however, came the gift of grace. God entered your personality at its deepest level when you were baptised, and he transformed you. He gave you a sublime goal to aim at and dream about, which is what St Thomas would call 'beatitude'. Robert Louis Stevenson called it the 'great task of happiness'. St Augustine said, 'We all want to be happy. Everyone will agree with me before the words are out of my mouth . . . so let us see if we can find the best way to achieve it.' Fulfilment in God's company, fulfilment for every fibre and atom of our being, that's the long-term goal of our existence, even though, paradoxically, we achieve it by forgetting ourselves and seeking the happiness of others. God said to you, 'I'm not some kind of ringmaster, cracking the whip and making you do tricks. I am your loving Father, and I have given you, too, the power to love, because you are a spark from the great fire which is me. I am inviting you to use all that autonomy, self-determination and freedom in a loving way; in other words to follow the path home to me, home to true fulfilment.' God's voice is the loving, urgent appeal to a grown-up person to use their freedom for the best and not to waste it. Not the bark of a sadistic sergeant major who can only make soldiers efficient by humiliating them.

This is what Paul is talking about in Galatians. He contrasts the lot of children and of slaves. Do you remember, years ago, there was a series on TV called *Upstairs, Downstairs*? It compared the life of the servants with the life of the family. The servants simply do what they are told. They sit around in the basement and wait for the bell to ring. The children of the family have infinitely greater freedom, to question, to argue. They have the freedom of the house. They can run along corridors and sing in the bath. Along with the freedom, however, goes the expectation that they will internalise their father's will and make it their own, that they will not just obey his orders but interpret them, and sometimes even anticipate them, and that they will do all this out of love and not out of compulsion. In the end, love will deliver more than imposed authority ever can. Remember Galatians 4:4: 'But when the fullness of time had come, God sent his Son, born of a woman, born under the law, in order to redeem those who were under the law, so that we might receive adoption as children.' He sent us Jesus to bring us up out of the basement, where there is no true freedom, into the Father's house, where there is. And Galatians 5:1: 'For freedom Christ has set us free. Stand firm, therefore, and do not submit again to a yoke of slavery.'

And there's the key to it. Slavery. The opposite of freedom is not obedience; it is slavery. We are called to do the will of our Father, and slavery is contrary to the will of our Father. Romans 8:15: 'For you did not receive a spirit of slavery to fall back into fear, but you have received a spirit of adoption. When we cry, "Abba! Father!" it is that very Spirit bearing witness with our spirit that we are children of God.' One of my jobs, then, is to examine my life to see whether I am still enslaved. Is part of me still in the basement? Have I totally accepted adoption as God's son?

What enslaves us is sin, and deceit. Read John 8:31-35: 'If you continue in my word, you are truly my disciples; and you will know the truth, and the truth will make you free . . . Very truly, I tell you, everyone who commits sin is a slave to sin. The slave does not have a permanent place in the household; the son has a place there forever.' Sin and deceit enslave. How do they worm their way into my life?

By pride, certainly. Pride makes us paint ourselves into a corner and stay there, out of sheer perversity of will. Pride leads to schism in the Church, an inability to say, 'I was wrong' or 'Now I see something I didn't see before.' Pride leads to breakdown in peace efforts (Northern Ireland, the Middle East). Pride engenders fear of apparent climbdown. It makes us defend a point of view long after we know in our heart that we're wrong. It is the quality of macho boys in the playground, but the macho boys turn into macho men, and don't grow out of it. It looks virtuous but is in fact vicious.

And then, by addiction. We can get addicted to people and to things. We can suffer from a fatal weakening of the will. Sooner or later you will come across the tragedy of a married man who is having an affair with another man's wife, and he knows that for everyone's sake he should break it off, but he cannot summon up the energy or the resolution to do so. Tragedy is the only word for it. Addiction saps the will. If we are unable to escape an addiction, we often end up justifying it, or denying it. This is where the deceit comes in. This is notoriously true of people who are hooked on alcohol: they can be so deceptive, even with themselves. Addiction to all kinds of drugs is clearly ruinous. And so, in a different way, is addiction to pornography, on or off the internet. An American spiritual director once said to me, 'Internet pornography is the crack cocaine of pornography', meaning, 'It is instantly addictive, and appallingly dangerous.' What St Paul says to the Galatians is so obviously right for us too: 'Stand firm, then, and do not submit again to a yoke of slavery.' That's got to be our overall principle. I claim my freedom.

Sin worms its way into my life, too, by resentment. Resentment contradicts the folly of the Cross, by which we live. The folly of the Saviour who was pinned to the Cross and forgave his killers. If I choose another path, that of resentment, I part company with the Gospel in a major way. Priests do this sometimes: they work up a great hatred of the bishop over an unfortunate appointment, or an imagined slight, or a bit of bad temper, or a careless remark. Priests can become bitter about their fellow clergy and refuse to go to the Chrism Mass, or Deanery meetings. People harbour grudges for long, long periods. There's a lovely story about a priest taking over a parish in the north of Norfolk – in fact two parishes in one, each with its own parish council. He discovered that they were not on speaking terms, but no one would tell him why. After six months he took the chairman of one of the councils down to the pub and loosened his tongue with a couple of pints. 'I'll tell you how that is, Father,' said the chairman. 'In 978 when the Vikings were comin', those blighters in that other village, they knew all about that, and they never told us.' A long time to nurse a grudge. When we give in to this, we abdicate our freedom.

And finally, the demon of envy and jealousy. Other people's promotion, other people's possessions, other people's natural gifts, can engender in me sarcasm, coldness, inverted snobbery. All these things are poison. So is the neurotic taking of offence – what my first boss used to call 'that delicious hurt feeling'. They are ways the Devil gets at us. They too are a terrible wound to our human freedom. If you compare yourself, unfavourably and obsessively, with other people, you are not free. If you allow yourself to be crucified by imagined slights, you are not free. Your claim to greatness is that you are God's beloved, and that you are filled with his Spirit. Why should you envy anyone else? And why should you allow yourself to be handicapped by self-imposed shackles? Claim your freedom.

In 1955 I was walking through Durham City with a prison visitor. We saw a group of prisoners working on the road. There did not seem to be anyone supervising them. 'Won't they escape?' I asked. 'Why, no,' he replied, 'that lot are so institutionalised that if you accidentally locked them out they would be hammering on the door to be let back in.' In our chronic weakness we can collude at our own imprisonment. We slip into obsessive ways of doing things: hypochondria, free-floating anxiety, scrupulous worry and behaviour, brittle and invariable insistence on our own timetable. The sadness is that in all these ways we inflict wounds on our own liberty.

To emphasise the law of freedom in Paul is not to advocate moral anarchy. Paul is not saying, 'Let rip, because there aren't any more rules.' He is saying, 'Change your mindset, so that the good actions you might once have done out of fear, you now do willingly and freely out of love, because you have received the Spirit of the living God.' The Church decrees for us a moral code, but she does not intend thereby to reproduce the Jewish Law. The Jewish Law gave you information about 623 ways in which you might sin, but no help in remaining virtuous. The Law of Christ, on the other hand, is the gift of the Holy Spirit, who gives us a hunger for happiness with God and the appetite and power to do his will. In Psalm 146 you find the line 'The Lord sets the prisoners free', and Augustine in his commentary on this says, 'For the little ones whom you see carried in their mothers' arms cannot yet walk, and are already in fetters; for they have received from Adam what they are loosened from by Christ.'* Commenting on the raising of Lazarus and the command of Jesus, 'Unbind him and let him go free', Augustine says, 'When the dead man had come forth, still bound; confessing, but guilty still; that his sins also might be taken away, the Lord said to his servants, "Loose him, and let him go." What does he mean by such words? Whatsoever ye loose on earth shall be loosed in heaven.'† Augustine sees the Church not as the inhibitor of Christian freedom, but as its agent.

Once you have acquired this way of seeing things, you sense a great release of spiritual energy. You experience, perhaps for the first time, self-respect and quiet self-confidence. You experience peace, because you have disposed of the harpies and furies which made your life a misery. At the same time you feel a great impatience with anything that stands in the way of your spiritual development. If I am made for beatitude, for ultimate happiness, I want the things that will contribute to it, and I adamantly refuse the things that distract me or halt my progress. The image of travelling light is a help. Do you remember Jesus saying, 'I am the gate of the sheepfold'? And in another place, 'Strive to enter through the narrow gate'? To get into the kingdom of heaven we have to be Jesus-shape, not encumbered with the baggage of self-pity, addiction, resentment, envy, obsession or pride. If we are carting that stuff with us, we'll get stuck in the opening to the kingdom. We have to know how to let go of things. And this is freedom.

---

* St Augustine, Tractatus 41 in Joannem
† St Augustine, Tractatus 49 in Joannem

11

Confession

A little girl comes home from church, and her father, who did not go with her, asks 'What was the sermon about?' The girl replies, 'Sin.' 'And what did the Vicar have to say about sin?' She thinks for a moment and says, 'He was against it.' To make sense of confession you have to be at home with the concept of sin. This is counter-cultural: the idea of moral guilt and accountability goes against the present grain of Western European civilisation. It causes quite a lot of lip-curling on the part of the media, as if there were something creepy and obscurantist even in talking about it. Now you and I are children of our age, and we have imbibed and inhaled the ambiguities of our society. Our parents and grandparents were different; they were given, and accepted, rules of thumb: if you do this, or that, then it's a sin; and if there is grave matter, and full awareness of what you are doing, and full consent of the will, then it's a mortal sin, a killer. The average Catholic did not always handle this material very easily, and sometimes erred on the black side and confessed as grave sin stuff which wasn't sinful at all, because it wasn't anyone's fault. A caricature of this would be the following, imaginary, conversation between a priest and penitent:

'I missed Mass on Sunday.'

'Was it your own fault? Could you have managed to go?'

'No, Father, I was in hospital having an emergency operation.'

'Then it's not a sin, and you don't have to confess it.'

'Well, I'm an old-fashioned Catholic, and I don't agree with you, and anyway I'd rather say it to be on the safe side.'

This conversation could be prolonged indefinitely. The priest could have asked, 'What kind of God do you believe in, if you honestly think he would punish you for being in hospital on Sunday?' He could have said, 'The Church has never actually taught what you believe.' All kinds of things he could have said, and it wouldn't have made a blind bit of difference. This good Catholic had taken on board, in his infancy, a wickedly oversimplified bit of moral theology, and the mind had closed. The fact that he made a nonsense of a valuable truth did not, however, evacuate the truth of meaning. What our parents and grandparents learned about mortal and venial sin, if properly taught and properly understood, was right. Unfortunately the oversimplified misunderstandings brought the whole idea of sin into disrepute. Middle-aged people sometimes speak critically today – critically and wistfully – about 'What the nuns taught us', or perhaps against what they *think* the nuns taught them.

When *Humanae Vitae* broke over our heads in 1968, and the principle of 'obeying your conscience before anything else' began to be widely quoted, people rushed to the opposite extreme and began to question all objective standards of morality. 'If the Church cannot get between my conscience and God, then of what value is the Church's moral guidance on anything? Surely, isn't the ultimate criterion how the individual feels, in him or herself, about actions and patterns of behaviour?' This question has been in the air now for the past 30 years or more. We have become progressively more and more individualist, more and more independent, more and more resentful of ethical pointers from any agency, especially the Church. In other words, we invent our own morality. The Pope talked about this in *Veritatis Splendor.** Well, these 30 years have been the formative years for many of us. It would be surprising if these trends had left us untouched. Steadily, the concept of sin has been eroding around us. Think of those

* Encyclical of John Paul II, *Veritatis Splendor* (1993)

who are cheerfully cohabiting. They're in no way wicked people, or bad people. They are not so much immoral as amoral. Moral statements have become irrelevant for them, like the answers to the questions no one is asking. And as the concept of sin has eroded, the Sacrament of Reconciliation, the tradition of penance, which was as old as the Church, has been eroding with it.

And yet, in our brave new millennium, if you reflect on it, it is clear that sin is alive and flourishing, and on a vast scale. The trials at the Hague for the Srebrenica massacre make your blood run cold. The cases of thousands of Rwandans burned to death in churches are still being processed. The enslavement of countless Eastern European girls sold into prostitution in our sophisticated cities is a crime crying to heaven for vengeance. The rate of abortion in our countries is monumental, and taken for granted, but nonetheless horrific. Rich and powerful people commit perjury without batting an eyelid and unjustly collect huge damages for libel. Corruption in high places is routine and hardly causes comment any more. The drug traffic is a prime example of unscrupulous people lining their pockets at the expense of shattered and tortured lives. The North Koreans are paying their debt to the Russians by exporting forced labourers to Siberia, if the media are to be believed. Recent events in Afghanistan show how sadistic and merciless human beings can be. The world is awash with injustice.

It's not hard to identify sin when it's on the news, or on the front page of the paper, and in general when it's being committed by somebody else, in a fairly spectacular form. We can say, virtuously, 'Well, I don't do any of those things' or 'There's none of that in my neighbourhood', as if that means that sin, if it exists, is all *out there,* away from me, nothing to do with me. 'No ethnic cleansing in Muswell Hill.' But we share a human nature with the people who *do* do these things. It would be astonishing if the fault-lines which make them live so badly were not also present in us. We

82

would be purblind if we pretended that the instincts of self-ishness, cruelty, exploitation and lust had entirely passed us by. You and I are children of Adam as well as children of God.

The whole of Catholic theology groups around the existence of sin. The Incarnation and Redemption are a response to human sin. The significance of the Crucifixion and Resurrection is entirely lost if we don't need rescuing. The whole sense of the Eucharist is summed up by the words of institution: 'This is the cup of my blood, the blood of the new and everlasting covenant, which will be shed for you and for all, so that sins may be forgiven.' How many times in the Gospel does Jesus say, 'Go in peace, your sins are forgiven'? To construct a religion of sweetness and light where there is no dark underside to life is quite insane. Sin is a major factor in human experience. It is a universal phenomenon. Only ostriches can pretend otherwise.

Now for the good news! As Catholics we can look this horror in the eye, because forgiveness is so easily accessible. '*O felix culpa*,' sings the Exultet at Easter – 'O happy sin of Adam!' I can risk naming my sins because the sacrament is there, and just as many of my sins are tangible, audible things, so the forgiveness of the Lord is tangible and audible. In this context, the context of this sacrament, we can call things by their proper names, and not go into denial about them. The Sacrament of Reconciliation is a superb and powerful contribution to our spiritual health. It liberates us to try again. It strikes off the shackles of the past. It is also an antidote to exaggerated independence (we mentioned this a moment ago), because it reconciles us to God by reconciling us to our fellow-Christians, to the Church. When the priest says, 'I absolve you' he is saying, *inter alia,* 'I receive you back into the communion of saints, which includes all your fellow-Christians.' Of course, the odds are that you have not actually fallen out of communion, and therefore in the radical sense don't need reconciling; but it may well be that your sense of Church, your sense of belonging, needs reinforcement. The Sacrament of Penance provides this.

Another thing confession does is remind us that God is, and always has been, full of forgiveness. In our darker moments we may have constructed for ourselves a picture of a cold, punitive, vengeful God, or a God who says, '*Me ne frego*' – 'I don't give a damn' – and washes his hands of us. The secular world, if it believes in God at all, reduces him to this kind of mechanistic power and nothing more. That's the way *we* sometimes treat one another, with brittleness and coolness and without sympathy. So not for nothing do we speak of 'celebrating' forgiveness: we celebrate the fact that God is not the monster of our pessimism and despair, not built in our image and likeness, not a kind of cosmic juggernaut, but he's the Father of Jesus Christ, he's Abba. The Pope began *Dives in Misericordia** by saying, 'It is God who is rich in mercy whom Jesus Christ has revealed to us as Father.' In the same letter he analyses the parable of the Prodigal Son and the real meaning of mercy. 'This love,' he says, 'is able to reach down to every prodigal son, to every human misery, and above all to every form of moral misery, to sin. When this happens, the person who is the object of mercy does not feel humiliated but rather found again, and restored to value.' (no. 6)

'Every prodigal son.' If we are depressed about our own track record, we tacitly add 'except me'. If we find it hard to forgive ourselves, we also find it hard to credit God with the understanding and the mercy which he undoubtedly has. This is a mistake. We have to let the tidal wave of God's comprehending love in, not keep it dammed up at the door.

And a bit later on, specifically about confession, the Pope says, 'In this sacrament each person can experience mercy in a unique way, that is, the love which is more powerful than sin.' (no. 13)

It's all about love. When we go to confession we put ourselves in the way of the torrential mercy of this phenomenal Lord, and learn from him, on the rebound, how to be merciful

---

* Encyclical of John Paul II, *Dives in Misericordia* (1980)

ourselves. Our poor world desperately needs large doses of mercy, whenever human beings get together and converse or negotiate or plan together: not icy justice, but mercy. The best person to practise mercy is the forgiven penitent. He knows what it's about.

Forgive me now if I say some very elementary things. A brief lunge into the Catechism, so to speak. I know that quite a number of readers will be converts, or have come into full communion with the Catholic Church as adults. You haven't had confession as an easy and automatic part of your infant and adolescent life. Others of you, maybe, while cradle Catholics, have somehow missed out on this aspect of the Church's life, and only came to terms with it later. It is different, taking this sacrament on board as already grown-up people, and sometimes difficult as well. Let me say, then, some things that are obvious, but still need saying, and periodically repeating.

First, the seal of confession. Whatever you say to the priest is utterly and totally secret, it is the best-kept secret in the world; you can totally trust the seal of confession. Indeed, the confessor often forgets what he has heard, and offends the penitent who returns after a month and says, 'Father, you remember what I told you . . .' and the poor priest has to say, 'Just remind me, would you . . .?'

Next, about the priest who hears your confession. He is a penitent himself. He is not judging you from a position of moral superiority. He is a fellow-sinner. By confessing your sins you are not humiliating yourself in his regard. We have to be big enough and wise enough to overcome our natural embarrassment with respect to our sins, whatever they are. To be hung up on such embarrassment, and therefore to go seldom or never to confession, is not worthy of us. 'If the sick person is too ashamed to show his wound to the doctor, the medicine cannot heal what it does not know.' That's the Council of Trent in 1551, quoting St Jerome in the fourth century. (Clearly, human nature does not change a great deal.) The priest in confession is as much a professional as the doctor in his surgery. This is a privileged forum where we can say anything, disclose anything.

Next, when we say, 'I will not sin again' we are not prophesying about the future, no one can do that; we are simply saying, 'I will try, and I mean that sincerely.' It is good to have a short act of contrition as part of your repertoire, which includes some such formula ('by the help of your grace I will not sin again'), unless you prefer to express your sorrow in your own words. Repentance is about the future, not the past. It's about how, with the grace of God, I plan to be different.

Then, finally, you may wonder what to say: is it about staccato words and actions which were wrong, or is it more about identifying the patterns of sin in your life and the roots of it? Well, I suppose it's both. It's viewing the event but trying to put it in a context. Some of our sins are also crosses which we carry, and it is not always easy to identify the place where the cross stops and the sin starts: we can leave that problem to God. The big context, of course, and I return to this without any apology, is that you are dealing directly with a supremely merciful God who wants nothing better than to put his arm round your shoulder and melt your fears with his love.

12

Lent

Is there a special 'Lenten way of being' which we should try to acquire? I believe that there most certainly is. It is not a miserable way of being, or a seeking of suffering for its own sake. Lent has its own brand of joy, but it is a deep and slightly austere joy, a sober joy. It comes from daring to face the truth, about God and ourselves. It comes from putting ourselves in training, so that we are more spiritually responsive, and sensitive to the voice of God. It comes from objectively identifying just where sin is, and what needs to be done about it. It comes from wrenching our attention away from our private concerns, from seeing ourselves as part of a universal and evangelising Church, and actually caring about the Body of Christ, its health and its growth, realising we have a part to play in this. It comes from confronting the desert, calling its bluff, and finding God at the heart of it. Let's see if we can unwrap some of this.

We know what Lent is all about. It does not stand by itself. It is preparation for Easter. It only makes sense with reference to Easter. It is the mind of the Church that through the liturgy we should re-live the salient facts of our salvation. Well, the peak of the liturgy is Easter. At Easter we re-live *the* salient fact of our salvation. The fact that I am saved, redeemed, with my sins forgiven, and gates of heaven open to me, is all because of Easter. Baptism gets its power from Easter. I have died to the world, and been buried with Christ, and with him I rose again. I am a new person. And it's all because of Easter. So even if we take great care during Lent not to sing Alleluia, it is only right that our thoughts should constantly be on Easter.

Well, it's no good bouncing all this on me for the first time on Easter Sunday morning. It's no good saying, out of the blue, 'Let your thought be on heavenly things, not on things that are on the earth, because you have died, and now the life you have is hidden with Christ in God.' It's no good saying out of the blue, 'Christ, our Passover, has been sacrificed. Let us celebrate the feast, then, by getting rid of all the old yeast of evil and wickedness, having only the unleavened bread of sincerity and truth.' Isaac Watts, in his *Moral Songs* has this immortal verse,

> 'Tis the voice of the sluggard: I heard him complain
> 'You have waked me too soon, I must slumber again.'

How tragic if, when Easter comes, I find myself saying, 'You have waked me too soon.' I think of the parable about the Master returning in the middle of the night, and finding the servants awake and ready. It is important for me, when Easter comes, to be an alert servant. 'Awake, O sleeper, and rise from the dead, and Christ shall give you light.' Now I am by nature a slow and sluggish man, and I need time to come round to seeing reality in the light of Easter. Lent gives me the chance. Lent invites me to see things as they really are. An example. The introduction of the euro to the twelve countries of Europe demanded a fair degree of softening-up, and oft-repeated information, and bits of practice, too. Otherwise the populations of the various countries would have been quite unprepared, and the new currency a disaster. Well, Lent is my softening-up time, so that I shall be ready for Easter.

If we make sacrifices and deny ourselves during Lent, we do it in the service of the truth. Discipline of all kinds helps to clear the mind, so that we can look steadily at the truth without distraction. If we satisfy our senses all the time, the vision gets clouded. We become chronically short-sighted. This reaches its extreme in addiction, where junkies can't see beyond the next fix, and alcoholics beyond the next drink. The pathos of this is not just the depth of human degradation it involves: it is, tragically, a denial of the truth. For reality consists in so much more than this. It is more than the next episode of *Eastenders* or the next package holiday on Ibiza. As a Christian, I need to be in command of the great underlying truths of my existence. To discern these truths it is necessary to keep in trim. Here is Leo the Great, preaching on the Third Sunday of Lent, quite possibly in St Peter's, about 1570 years ago:

> As you are about to celebrate the Paschal Festival, dearly beloved, let you so exercise yourselves in these sacred absti-nences, that you may approach the most holy feast free from every disorder. Let the spirit of pride, from which all sins have come, be driven out by the spirit of humility; and let those who are puffed up with arrogance become mild through forbearance. Let those whom some insult has provoked, becoming reconciled, seek earnestly to return to the peace of friendship.*

'Free from every disorder.' Lent, with its call to self-denial, keeps me in trim. We are not all gymnasts or athletes. We know, however, that the training and exercise done by gymnasts and athletes bring them great satisfaction, because they have the sense of employing their body to its full potential, the sense of a body in perfect working order. Well, I need to employ my soul to its full potential, and I need to have a soul in perfect working order, because then I can come to grips with the things that really matter, and are really true. How pathetic if I live the whole of my human existence anaesthetised with bread and circuses, and never focusing on the reason for my existence. The old catechism used to say, 'God made me to know him, to love him and to serve him in this world, and to be happy with him for ever in the next.' To perceive this truth, and live by it, I have to make sure my other desires are on the leash. The self-denial of Lent can bring the same sense of satisfaction that the gymnast experiences, as I feel my

---

* PL54, c.285, Serm. 44, Quad. 6

spirit unfold. As a member of the human race I am equipped to know truth: let me use the equipment, and use it to the maximum.

I am equipped to know truth. The truth that towers above all other truths, and lies at the root of them all, is that I am man under God, not man going it alone and answerable only to himself. My status is that of man under God. God knows me individually, knows me by name, and he loves me. He loves me so much that he has shared his Son with me; for the sake of his Son he has adopted me, and has invited me to spend eternity by his side. My conscious self is not doomed to go out like a spent candle. I am immortal. 'To be happy with him for ever in the next.' That's the fact before which all other facts have to give way. That's the priority. If, in the course of the year, this fact gets obscured by other matters, by more trivial and passing happinesses, then Lent is a blessed time, because it allows me to set my spiritual and mental house in order, do that vital readjustment which brings things into their true proportion.

I can, of course, wilfully blind myself to this truth, and waste my life on what are really unsubstantial incidentals, and chuck away my immortality. I can do this by a life of sin. The temptations to do this are very strong, and very plausible. If we deny or overlook the existence of sin we are stupid, and playing into the Devil's hand. Let's face it, anyone who is try-ing to live as God wills is bound to be sorely tempted, and sometimes in insidious ways. It stands to reason that this will be so. Lucifer is, after all, blindingly intelligent, and he infallibly finds the chink in our armour. It is as sure that we shall be tempted as it was, at the height of the London Blitz, that the sirens would sound over the East End, and all the families would have to pile into the Underground or the shelters in their back gardens. To pretend that it wasn't happening would have been, quite simply, perverse. If we pretend that our lives are somehow withdrawn from the possibility of temptation and sin, or that to talk about temptation and sin is naïve and juvenile, we too are perverse, and what's more we are in danger. Sin isn't an old-fashioned or outmoded concept. The self-denial of Lent stops us being perverse. It helps us to see things as they are, and call them by their proper names. It saves us from the fate of the house in Luke 6:46-49, the one which collapsed because it was built on sand.

It would be a pity if we saw the self-denial of Lent as a way of clawing ourselves up to heaven. The goodness of God is great, and it is wholly gratuitous. Heaven cannot be earned; it can only be received gratefully as a free gift. So whatever effort we make during Lent isn't about gaining entitlement to something. 'He owes me one.' No he doesn't, he owes me nothing, and I shall never be other than a suppliant before God, an asker. The self-denial of Lent, however, disposes me to recognise the gift when it is offered, recognise it and accept it in full. In Luke 19 Jesus weeps over Jerusalem, and he says, 'Would that even today you knew the things that make for peace! But now they are hid from your eyes.' That's the RSV translation. However, the Greek doesn't just say 'that make for peace' – '*pros eirenen*'; it says '*pros eirenen sou*', meaning 'the things that make for *your* peace.' How many times Christ must have wept over me, and said, 'If only you had the sense to see that your present way of acting won't ever bring you peace. If only you could see the things that *would* help you find true and lasting peace.' Lent is the time for discovering and discerning those things, and having the courage to ditch the rest. 'Repent and believe the Gospel' is one of the formulae for imposing the ashes. 'Repent' is the same as 'Be converted'. Conversion is not too strong a word. Be converted from small-scale self-indulgence to large-scale generosity, towards God and towards others. Be converted from thinking you've got it taped, be converted to realising that the generosity is all on God's side. The three great Lenten gospels of year A are large-scale, generous, majestic gospels. The Woman at the Well is about water as a sign of the over-whelming grace of God. The Man Born Blind is about the life-transforming gift of faith. The Raising of Lazarus is about eternal life being offered to us. They're not about piffling little things like not taking sugar in your tea. They're about the great underlying skeletal issues, like the shape of my life, and how I owe it all to God.

Lent may feel very personal, but it is also profoundly ecclesial. All over the country, in big parishes and small, since September, enquirers have become catechumens, and cate-chumens have met their bishop and have been put by him on the final stage of their entry into the Church. Now their sights are set on Holy Saturday night. Some of them will be baptised. Adult baptism is something beautiful and moving beyond words. Most of them will be received into full communion and confirmed. All of them will receive their First Communion at the Vigil Mass. The Rite of Christian Initiation is an official liturgical document of the Catholic Church. Much research has been done on the patristic history of it. This study suggests that in the final weeks, that is the weeks of Lent, the candidates should cease formal instruction and, so to speak, coast home on the prayers of the faithful. It's the time for the Holy Spirit to do his thing. Not that the Spirit has been absent from all the previous experiences and doctrinal instructions; of course he hasn't. But at this point, as Lent starts, human beings ideally stand back and commend the prospective converts quite simply to the mercy of God, that God will enlighten them and illumine them as only he can, and in ways we poor wordy people cannot express. Only in this way will they be prepared for the gift of faith on Easter morning. The best analogy I have heard is that of the Tall Ships Race from Devon to Rhode Island in the United States. The Rhode Islanders know when the leaders in the race are likely to appear over the horizon, and, as soon as they do so, the Americans set out in a fleet of little boats to meet the great yachts. They sail up to them, turn round, and escort them into harbour with much hooting of sirens, cheer-ing, and uncorking of champagne bottles. It's a festival for everyone. In Lent we go out to meet those who are becoming members of the Church, and accompany them into harbour, above all by praying for them. Several hundred new Catholics in the UK, this Easter, will be enriched and strengthened if you offer your Lent for them. One or two of these new Catholics will become great leaders in the Church. It is all in the providence of God. This is a moment of prophetic growth, and you can contribute to it by making an unselfish Lent. That's how the Body of Christ works. Remember the Letter to the Ephesians (4:15):

> If we live by the truth and in love,
> we shall grow in all ways into Christ, who is the head,
> by whom the whole body is fitted and joined together,
> every joint adding its own strength,
> for each separate part to work according to its function.
> So the body grows,
> until it has built itself up, in love.

'So the body grows.' If I make a good Lent, I shall be a joint adding my own strength, so that the body may grow and build itself up. The growth of the Catholic Church in England and Wales is above all a spiritual thing, and my contribution to it must be above all a spiritual one. Lent is when I can feed in something worthwhile.

Finally, Lent begins in the desert. This is where Jesus meets, and overcomes, temptation. The desert is a privileged place in Christian spirituality. In our lives, there must be space for silence and solitude. We need to lay ourselves open, in humility, to the saving action of God. This requires protracted peace and quiet. God says in Hosea 2:14, 'I will take her out into the desert and speak to her heart.' In the desert we sometimes feel bored, and fidgety. This is a challenge from the Lord to stay with it, and not head back for the bright lights and the noise. The mystery of God is encountered when we relinquish the normal props of life, and look steadily and patiently into the darkness which surrounds him. Listen to this quotation from *The Cloud of Unknowing*:

When you first begin you find only darkness and as it were a cloud of unknowing. You don't know what this means except that in your will you feel a steadfast intention reaching out towards God . . . reconcile yourself to wait in this darkness as long as is necessary, but still go on longing after him whom you love.*

This Lent, may your spirit cry out to him whom you love.

---

* *The Cloud of Unknowing* (Anon, fourteenth century), translated by Clifton Wolters (Penguin, 1961)

13

'Mary Immaculate'

'Mary Immaculate, Star of the Morning.' This is the first line of a hymn. It used to make me wild when I was a seminarian in the 1950s. I could not understand the notion of the Immaculate Conception. I had come from a Protestant public school with a heavily rationalistic outlook and a curling lip. Devotion to Mary, Italian-style, seemed to me at that time to be so much candyfloss. I couldn't get into it. It was sentiment without substance. I remember that during the Marian Year in 1954, which saw a flurry of dedications, consecrations and crownings of statues, an Italian bishop turned up in the College wanting a translator for a pamphlet he had just written about the woman in the Apocalypse with the stars round her head. He identified this, of course, with Our Lady. The number twelve, too, as you might guess, had an occult significance. It seemed to me that the whole thing was pretty average non-sense, and in addition he wanted not a version in educated English, but a literal, word-for-word translation. It all went to confirm my worst suspicions: when it comes to Mary, the Catholic Church goes completely dotty, loses touch with proper theology and even proper language, and descends to inarticulate billing and cooing.

Which all goes to show how priggish and immature I was. The years between have made me, I hope, much wiser. Mary is an integral part of God's project for the world, and also of his project for the Church. Without her, it would look completely different. The fact is that God knows us, through and through. He knows that if the Church were left entirely to men, we would turn it into a heartless barracks, where people threaten and bark at one another all day long. If the Church were left entirely to men, we would wreck it. We would fill it with male concepts, ultimatums, hard rough edges, insensitivities. We don't do too badly as it is. Balthasar says in *Elucidations*: 'And because in this manly-masculine world, all that we have is one ideology replacing another, everything becomes polemical, critical, bitter, humourless, and ultimately boring, and people in their masses run away from such a Church.'*

I remember about ten years ago going to the seminary in Sydney (which was called, incidentally, Manly) to talk to the priests of the diocese. The seminarians had gone home, but the notices were still on the board. One of them was from the MC, and it read, 'Here is the list of Mass-servers for this week. If anyone changes the names on this list, I will break his legs.' I have a soft spot for Oz humour. Charming, isn't it?

However! Because God has given us Mary to be our mother, to be mother of the Church and model of the Church, those sharp edges of ours are blunted by something else: compassion. There is another strain of awareness in the Church which is to do with intimacy, with sympathy, with comprehension, with patience, with contemplative reflection. We, rather carelessly, attribute maleness to all three Persons of the Trinity. God realises how lopsided our understanding is, and Mary is there, not to be a fourth person of the Trinity, not to be a goddess, but to be a filter, so that we can experience through her not just the justice and the power of God but also his tenderness. Through her we discover that God is as much feminine as he is masculine. We need daily convincing that, here on earth, great strength and heroism can be combined with gentleness, great patience and a capacity for suffering. Mary teaches us this, not by what she says but by what she is. She is a vital part of God's Providence for us. She saves us from being a totally macho Church.

---

* Hans Urs von Balthasar, *Elucidations* (SPCK, London, 1975), a translation of *Klarstellungen: zur Prüfung der Geister* (Verlag Herder, Freiburg im Breisgau, 1971)

Christianity minus Mary is a stark thing. Here is a very fine poem by R. S. Thomas, called 'In Church':

Often I try
To analyse the quality
Of its silences. Is this where God hides
From my searching? I have stopped to listen,
After the few people have gone,
To the air recomposing itself
For vigil. It has waited like this
Since the stones grouped themselves about it.
These are the hard ribs
Of a body that our prayers have failed
To animate. Shadows advance
From their corners to take possession
Of places the light held
For an hour. The bats resume
Their business. The uneasiness of the pews
Ceases. There is no other sound
In the darkness but the sound of a man
Breathing, testing his faith
On emptiness, nailing his questions
One by one to an untenanted cross.*

You feel man pitted against the emptiness, asking the pitiless Calvinist questions. In Catholic culture, he would have been aware, however confusedly, of the wise and motherly care of Mary whose maternal understanding can enfold even our doubts.

The importance of Our Lady, and the whole list of titles with which the Church adorns her, all stem from the fact that she is Mother. That's the heart of the matter. It is hard for those of us who are men to imagine what motherhood involves, the intensity of the bond which develops between

---

* *The Collected Poems of R. S. Thomas, 1945-1990* (J. M. Dent, 1993), originally published in *The Bread of Truth* (1963)

mother and child. To carry another person within your own body must be an incredible thing. To feed your own baby child must be an experience beyond description. The long years of upbringing are, clearly, the responsibility of both parents, but in the early and most formative years it is the mother who bears the brunt of this. She knows her child with a depth that no one else can match: body language, tones of voice, everything. Men have to be very humble in the face of this, and admit that we are incapable of comprehending fully what is involved, and the depth of feeling that a mother has for her child. The Incarnation means that the Son of God submitted himself to this process. He needed to be carried, fed and brought up and known in depth. And the person God trusted to do this was Mary.

In view of all this, what I am going to say now might seem a bit rough and a bit dismissive, and I assure you this is not meant to be the case. We have a respect and a gratitude and a love for our mothers, whether or not we still have them with us, that is hard to articulate, and this is right. Under God, we owe them more than words can ever describe. Nothing I say here is meant to detract from this.

But think of yourself growing up. Not so long ago. We grow like young saplings planted in the garden, don't we? If we are to grow straight, we need a stake beside us to support us. If the stake is weak and willowy, or if it falls over, then the sapling grows lopsided too. East Anglia, where I have lived for many years, is full of Scots pines. They are a bit like the Roman umbrella pines, but more gnarled and bent. They were never staked. They take the brunt of the east wind, and they adapt their shape to the gales that come in from the North Sea. In fact, no two Scots pines are the same shape: but all of them show signs of what they have been through. So do all saplings imperfectly staked. So do children. So do you. So do I. The adult I am stems from the child I was. My childhood was formed by parents, school and Church, but mainly by parents, and mainly by my mother. If she had hang-ups, she passed them down to me. If she was pessimistic and a bit depressive, she passed that down to me. If she found some members of her family defective in their duty and hard to forgive, she passed that down to me. If her self-esteem was low, she passed that down to me. I was like a sapling imperfectly staked. The adult I am shows signs of the upbringing I had, and the upbringing will not have been – cannot have been – perfect.

By and large, as we grow up, we learn to accept the negative things in our lives with resignation and courage. I am enormously impressed by primary school children who are diabetic, and who at certain times of day will slip away for a minute to inject themselves with insulin. They know it is unavoidable, even if other children don't have the same problem, and they quietly get on with it. These are the cards they have been dealt by life. I am enormously impressed with primary school children who are asthmatic, who have to fight for breath, and who carry a little inhaler with them for when breathing becomes impossible. There is a quiet heroism about these kids. They don't complain, because they know that it won't help. They just get on with it. It's the movement of their shoulders which betrays the daily battle the asthmatic children have to fight. It is as if, at the beginning of their lives, they had been issued with a haversack full of rocks, and told, 'Carry that.' And carry it they do – they have learned how to do it, and they do it well.

Well, there are haversacks full of other rocks. They afflict the soul more than the body, but are just as serious. What about a child who is told at a tender age, 'You're no good. You're a disappointment'? That lesson goes deep, and is internalised, and becomes a weight which has to be carried, possibly for a lifetime. In adult terms it turns into 'You're a failure. You're a fraud. If people knew what you were really like they wouldn't want to know you. You're just bluffing people. You're not really qualified to do anything or to be anything.' Insistent sabotaging voices, which so many adults carry in their heads, like cassette tapes which were put there when they were small, and have been playing ever since. Teachers do it to us; on occasion it is the Church which does it to us. Parents can do it to us without meaning to: it isn't deliberate. Sometimes they say to their children, 'I will love you so long as you're good. But if you're not good I won't love you any more.' It's just one more weapon in their disciplinary armoury: after all, how do you keep kids in order? But this particular weapon can trigger off in us a panicky passion for pleasing grown-ups, pleasing superiors, because the approval of these people is like oxygen – it isn't just nice, it is required for survival. The thought of being deprived of love or approval engenders anguish and, at the worst, despair in a child. We all know people who tend to ingratiate themselves with authority: well, this is where all that begins. Parents who never praise their children in an unqualified way can have the same effect, and all the time for laudable reasons: 'Your school report was good, but I was upset that you didn't do so well at history, or hockey: what a shame.' The effect of these innocent mistakes can stay with a person all their life long. Whatever success they have in business, whatever promotion they achieve in their profession, whatever scientific breakthrough they may effect, deep down the cassette is still playing: 'You're no good.' This is a load that many people carry for the whole of their lives: the suffering is invisible, but only too real. Here is another brilliant poem by R. S. Thomas. It's called 'Sorry'.

> Dear parents,
> I forgive you my life,
> Begotten in a drab town,
> The intention was good;
> Passing the street now,
> I see still the remains of sunlight.

It was not the bone buckled;
You gave me enough food
To renew myself.
It was the mind's weight
Kept me bent, as I grew tall.

It was not your fault.
What should have gone on,
Arrow aimed from a tried bow
At a tried target, has turned back,
Wounding itself
With questions you had not asked.*

Mary is for us a sign that self-contempt is not what God wants from us. Why do I say this? Because she was chosen and fashioned to be the mother of his Son. Her task was to bring him up in such a way that he would be the perfect model of human-ness. From her he learned tenderness; think of the way he treated women. From her he learned to speak slowly, eloquently, sincerely; think of the parables. From her he learned sympathy for the underdog, for lepers and immigrants and blind people; think of the woman taken in adultery. From her he learned how to survive disappointment, adversity, enmity; think of the Apostles letting him down, and of the implacable hostility of the religious establishment. From her he learned self-confidence and self-value; how else could he, a country man from Galilee with no special education, have addressed those large crowds of hearers with such assurance ('You have heard it was said of old . . . But I say to you . . .')? When God became man he entered the arena of human characteristics, yes. But it is impossible to imagine Christ as neurotic or misogynist or depressive or self-pitying. He was not those things because he had a superb mother. Psychologists talk about our need for a 'good enough

---

* *The Collected Poems of R. S. Thomas, 1945-1990* (J. M. Dent, 1993), originally published in *The Bread of Truth* (1963)

mother'. Jesus had a mother who was more than 'good enough', and she gave the world a son who was more than 'good enough'. She was superb, simply in order that he might be superb.

To make sure that she would be superb, the Father ordained that she should be conceived immaculate. Her human legacy to her son was of double importance, for she was his only human parent. The sad law of fallen human nature is that parents pass down to their children a certain number of blind spots, a certain amount of rubbish. 'Oh see, in guilt I was born, a sinner was I conceived' (Psalm 51:5). God's way of stopping this from happening to our divine Saviour was to arrest that process at the vital point in the chain. When Joachim and Anne conceived Mary, God intervened. He gave her a soul and a character which was totally innocent and totally undamaged. That's what the Immaculate Conception means, and it makes eminent good sense.

And it means, almost as a by-product, something stupendous for you and me. God gave us Mary at the foot of the Cross. She is to be a mother to us. She brings to bear all the wisdom and intuition that ordinary mothers have about their children, but this is a mother who does not damage her children by being absorbed in her own worries, or rather sparing in encouragement, or hypercritical of their efforts. She doesn't put us down. She does not transmit diffidence to us. She comprehends us, and she loves us, and we can ask her help with absolute confidence, even when we find it hard to verbalise our distress. Here is a paragraph from Bernanos' *Diary of a Country Priest* which shows just how special she is:

> The eyes of Our Lady are the only real child-eyes that have ever been raised to our shame and sorrow. Yes, to pray to her as you should you should feel those eyes of hers upon you: they are not indulgent – for there is no indulgence without something of bitter experience – they are eyes of gentle pity, wondering sadness, and with something more in them, never yet known or expressed, something which makes her younger

than sin, younger than the race from which she sprang, and though a mother, by grace, Mother of all grace, our little youngest sister.*

What this paragraph does not mention is her power, and her will to come to our aid when we feel crippled. Let's end this reflection with the most primitive, simple and eloquent prayer to Our Lady. It dates from the beginning of the third century.

We fly to thy protection, O holy Mother of God,
despise not our petitions in our necessities,
but deliver us from all danger,
O ever glorious and blessed Virgin.

---

* Georges Bernanos, *Diary of a Country Priest,* translated from *Le Journal d'un Curé de Campagne* (Librairie Plon, 1936)

14

The Eucharist and the World

'I don't watch the news any more, it is just too depressing.' Many people feel like this in today's world. More mass graves are discovered in Bosnia, more Rwandans accused of genocide, a kamikaze killer in Tel Aviv, a financial scandal in the city . . . the list is endless. The things that happen in our world are at the same time so painful and so massive that the well-intentioned individual feels helpless in the face of them.

In many parishes there is regular Exposition of the Blessed Sacrament and many devout people will come to the church for short or long periods, tranquilly kneeling and waiting. Before the monstrance on the altar they can say, 'Those things aren't going on here. Jesus is all that is merciful and pure.' They may see the Blessed Sacrament as a refuge from what is intolerable and unthinkable. There is a very respectable strand of spirituality which follows this line. Think of some of the traditional hymns we sing:

> Jesus who gave himself for you
> upon the cross to die
> opens to you his Sacred Heart,
> O to that heart draw nigh.

or

> Jesu, the very thought of thee
> with sweetness fills my breast;
> but sweeter far thy face to see
> and in thy presence rest.

There is nothing wrong with this kind of devotion: in order

to concentrate on the abiding presence of Christ, whether dwelling within us by baptism or enthroned in the Blessed Sacrament, we have to shut out extraneous concerns. In doing so, we become like the rifleman practising his markmanship at the butts. Between sessions, he rests his eyes on the green grass, because it is such a welcome change from straining forward at a tiny target. To think of Jesus brings relief: 'Come to me, all you who labour and are overburdened, and I will give you rest' (Matthew 11:28).

Religion, however, is not meant to be an alternative world; it is meant to be integrated with daily life, painful though this may be. Religion should never be a way of pushing reality under the carpet, simply because we find reality brutal and untameable. You see, that word 'exposed' can be understood in two ways. The Blessed Sacrament is exposed to our gaze for adoration – that's the obvious meaning. At her Golden Jubilee, the Queen rode in her golden coach through the streets of London so as to be seen and acclaimed by the crowds; it's the same idea. But the Blessed Sacrament is also exposed to the modern world, face to face with all its ambiguity and ugliness, reminding us of the truth of the Incarnation in which Christ confronted evil and overcame it. Becoming human meant that the Son of God exposed himself to the worst the world could do to him. Nazareth wasn't a bolt-hole. (Think of the number of Italian families who have 'Esposito' as their surname. I imagine that way back in the family tree there is someone who was an unwanted baby, and who was dumped in a basket on the doorstep of a convent or an orphanage: exposed to whatever the elements might do to him.) Jesus came to his own and his own received him not. He confronted the wayward world and put himself at its mercy, and in its own way the world took stock of who he was and tried to eliminate him. Indeed, it thought it had eliminated him. By submitting to this process he saved the world. One of the Fathers of the Church paints us the picture of Christ who makes himself the bait which the Devil devours, and by which the Devil is destroyed. That kind of exposure.

There is a link between the eucharistic Body of Christ and his Body which is the Church. It is hard to think of one without the other. The Church, however, is something of an enigma. On the one hand it is all those things Vatican II said it was: God's vineyard, God's field, his spouse, his pilgrim people, the prelude to the kingdom of heaven. On the other hand it is earthy and imperfect. It is vulnerable to sexual scandal, to financial scandal, to hypocrisy and careerism, to clerical cover-ups, to unkindness and exploitation. The Church is a great mystery. It is shot through with the divine, the recipient of divine guarantee. Simultaneously it is only too human, and sometimes you want to weep for the Church. It is not so long ago that it was castrating boy sopranos, executing criminals in the Papal States, being complacent about the slave trade. You wonder: 'Is the Church still only in its infancy? It seems that it has such a long way still to go before it measures up to the standards of the Gospel.' We can say this as loving members, without a shadow of disloyalty. It is hard to behold the Blessed Sacrament in the monstrance without thinking of the Church, and of how the Church fails to live up to its identity as the Body of Christ. If the Church was in all respects what it should be, it would be so attractive that people would be knocking our doors down all day and all night long, saying, 'I want to join. What must I do? Where do I sign?' The RCIA would be so oversubscribed that you would have to run it every evening of the week. This is, I regret to say, not the case. It is hard to worship the Sacred Host without praying for the Church.

Scripture has that lovely expression for God the Son throwing in his lot with us. 'He pitched his tent among men,' it says. In Exodus the Tent of Meeting was a rather grand affair, because it contained the Tabernacle. It was designer-built, and God was the designer. There were elaborate instructions for its erection. In the New Testament, however, Our Lord opts for a much more ordinary tent. If you have been to the Holy Land and have followed the road from Jerusalem down to the Jordan, you will recall the little settlements of Bedouin tents in the desert, low-slung goat-skin and camel-hide affairs without any glamour, quite the opposite of the splendid ones in which today Scandinavians invade Mediterranean watering-places. Jesus assumed human nature in its lowliest and simplest mode. That was his tent. He pitched his tent among us, and was indistinguishable from the rest of the *anawim*, the voice-less ones. He faced up to the mighty of the earth, the religious authorities and the Roman governor: eye-to-eye contact with Caiaphas and Pilate. From the standpoint of humility he engaged with the world. He took on the mess. Not just the exterior mess of fallen humanity, but the interior mess of Judas, his intimate, who should have known better. 'But it was you, my own brother . . . We walked together in the house of the Lord.' What is true of God Incarnate is true of the Blessed Sacrament. It is God's statement, where it is generally accepted that might is right, God's statement of fragility, God's expressing solidarity with ordinary people who are not at all mighty.

Did you ever see the film *The Mission*? It is about the eighteenth-century Jesuit settlements in South America, on the borders of Paraguay and Brazil, places where they did not just read the Gospel to people but tried to live it with them. The Jesuits fell foul of the colonial governments because they were giving the Guarani Indians a sense of their own dignity, and subtracting them from the slave market. The Spanish and Portuguese governments therefore put pressure on the Church authorities to close the settlements down. (They not only closed the settlements down – they closed the Jesuits down too, but that's another story.) The climax of the film is a grim shoot-out in which the Indians are massacred in their hundreds by superior fire-power. In the final scene the priest carries the Blessed Sacrament out of the burning church, and for a moment the soldiers hesitate to shoot him; but only for a moment, and then we see the monstrance tumbled in the dust. It is like a parable. Jesus took his chance by becoming man, faced extreme hostility and was tumbled in the dust. Philippians 2:8: 'And being found in human form, he humbled himself and became obedient to the point of death – even death on a cross. Therefore God also highly exalted him . . .' The Eucharist is our assurance that if we face up to the world in all its injustice and cynicism, however humble and helpless we may feel, God will give us the victory.

The Church, which is just as much the Body of Christ as the Sacred Host is, should dare to be exposed to the world without being contaminated by it. There is a Chinese game which children play sitting on the kerb. Three hand-signals for scissors, paper and stone. The game revolves around the question, 'What is the hardest, the most resistant? What can cut into what? How can you avoid being softer than your opponent?' We have to be able to sit on the kerb with the pagan world and dare to play, but not to be softer than it. We are supposed to be the leaven in the batch, the yeast which turns the dough into bread. To do its thing, the yeast has to allow itself to be inserted in the mix. But ultimately the yeast has to be stronger than the dough. If we are mousy and compliant about the vital issues which affect us all – pro-life issues, Third World economic issues, the right of children to religious education, the cynical promotion of the arms trade – we are being softer, we are being contaminated. The Eucharist should animate and strengthen us so that we dare to look utilitarian society in the eye and say, 'It will not do – people deserve better.' We in the Church receive the Body of Christ in order to become more authentically the Body of Christ, to present a courageous and saintly face to the world, not run away from it.

Many years ago a Passionist priest visited Rome. He was working in Sweden, and was one of the first foreign priests to settle there for any length of time. This was a new kind of missionary. In fact he had come to Rome to do a course in missiology, but he thought that it was a waste of time, because all the lectures were about Africa: no one seemed to have a clue about labouring as a missionary in post-Christian Europe. He and his colleagues had set up a parish in a market town some distance from Stockholm, and had begun to experience in a new way what it felt like to be irrelevant. Swedish society simply did not understand what they were about. It wasn't downright hostility, or the working-out of historical grudges. It was, if anything, a monumental boredom and lack of interest in what the Catholic Church stood for. This was coupled, of course, with a good dose of suspicion about anything which had to be imported. Life in Sweden was so good, so prosperous, and protected by a superb welfare state. What could the Church of Rome offer, or add? So, 'Not today, thank you, don't call us, we'll call you.' Then, one warm Sunday afternoon, the priests arranged Benediction for their tiny flock, and they left the door of the church open because it was hot. By the end, there was quite a group of Swedes clustered in the porch, watching intently, and some of them were crying. 'What's the matter?' asked the priest, and they replied, 'That's the most beautiful thing we have ever seen in our lives.' The music, the candles, the vestments, the reverence, but above all the mystery of the Eucharist had struck home, even in an unpretentious chapel in an unpretentious country High Street. The Eucharist *is* beautiful, and we are so incredibly fortunate to be the heirs to it. It speaks so powerfully and so eloquently.

May our world make its own what Luke 24:35 says about the men on the Road to Emmaus: 'Then they told what had happened on the road, and how he had been made known to them in the breaking of the bread.'

Acknowledgements

The publishers wish to express their gratitude to the following for permission to include copyright material in this book:

The Cloud of Unknowing, translated by Clifton Wolters (Penguin Classics, 1961). Copyright © Clifton Wolters, 1961.

Diary of a Country Priest, translated from *Le Journal d'un Curé de Campagne,* and published by Macmillan Inc, 1935. Copyright © Palgrave Macmillan.

Page 43. From article by Paul Murray in *Spirituality*, July/August 2002. Published by Dominican Publications, 42 Parnell Square, Dublin 1.

Sacred Reading by Michael Casey (Liguori/Triumph Publications, 1995). Copyright © Liguori/Triumph Publications.

Elucidations by Hans Urs von Balthasar (SPCK, London, 1975), a translation of *Klarstellungen: zur Prüfung der Geister* (Verlag Herder, Freiburg im Breisgau, 1971). Copyright © 1975, SPCK, London.

'In Church' and 'Sorry' from *The Collected Poems of R. S. Thomas, 1945-1990* (J. M. Dent, 1993), originally published in *The Bread of Truth* (1963). Copyright © J. M. Dent, 1993.

Every effort has been made to trace the owners of copyright material and it is hoped that no copyright has been infringed. Pardon is sought and apology made if the contrary be the case, and a correction will be made in any reprint of this book.